THE
BRONTËS

COMPREHENSIVE RESEARCH
AND STUDY GUIDE

BLOOM'S
MAJOR
NOVELISTS

EDITED AND WITH AN
INTRODUCTION BY HAROLD BLOOM

CURRENTLY AVAILABLE

BLOOM'S MAJOR DRAMATISTS

Anton Chekhov
Henrik Ibsen
Arthur Miller
Eugene O'Neill
Shakespeare's Comedies
Shakespeare'sHistories
Shakespeare's Romances
Shakespeare's Tragedies
George Bernard Shaw
Tennessee Williams

BLOOM'S MAJOR NOVELISTS

Jane Austen
The Brontës
Willa Cather
Charles Dickens
William Faulkner
F. Scott Fitzgerald
Nathaniel Hawthorne
Ernest Hemingway
Toni Morrison
John Steinbeck
Mark Twain
Alice Walker

BLOOM'S MAJOR SHORT STORY WRITERS

William Faulkner
F. Scott Fitzgerald
Ernest Hemingway
O. Henry
James Joyce
Herman Melville
Flannery O'Connor
Edgar Allan Poe
J. D. Salinger
John Steinbeck
Mark Twain
Eudora Welty

BLOOM'S MAJOR WORLD POETS

Geoffrey Chaucer
Emily Dickinson
John Donne
T. S. Eliot
Robert Frost
Langston Hughes
John Milton
Edgar Allan Poe
Shakespeare's Poems & Sonnets
Alfred, Lord Tennyson
Walt Whitman
William Wordsworth

BLOOM'S NOTES

The Adventures of Huckleberry Finn
Aeneid
The Age of Innocence
Animal Farm
The Autobiography of Malcolm X
The Awakening
Beloved
Beowulf
Billy Budd, Benito Cereno, & Bartleby the Scrivener
Brave New World
The Catcher in the Rye
Crime and Punishment
The Crucible

Death of a Salesman
A Farewell to Arms
Frankenstein
The Grapes of Wrath
Great Expectations
The Great Gatsby
Gulliver's Travels
Hamlet
Heart of Darkness & The Secret Sharer
Henry IV, Part One
I Know Why the Caged Bird Sings
Iliad
Inferno
Invisible Man
Jane Eyre
Julius Caesar

King Lear
Lord of the Flies
Macbeth
A Midsummer Night's Dream
Moby-Dick
Native Son
Nineteen Eighty-Four
Odyssey
Oedipus Plays
Of Mice and Men
The Old Man and the Sea
Othello
Paradise Lost
The Portrait of a Lady
A Portrait of the Artist as a Young Man

Pride and Prejudice
The Red Badge of Courage
Romeo and Juliet
The Scarlet Letter
Silas Marner
The Sound and the Fury
The Sun Also Rises
A Tale of Two Cities
Tess of the D'Urbervilles
Their Eyes Were Watching God
To Kill a Mockingbird
Uncle Tom's Cabin
Wuthering Heights

THE
BRONTËS

COMPREHENSIVE RESEARCH
AND STUDY GUIDE

BLOOM'S
MAJOR
NOVELISTS

**EDITED AND WITH AN INTRODUCTION
BY HAROLD BLOOM**

3 5 7 9 8 6 4

Library of Congress Cataloging-in-Publication Data

The Brontës / edited and with an introduction by Harold Bloom.
p.   cm.—(Bloom's major novelists)
Includes bibliographical references and index.
ISBN 0-7910-5257-5
1. Brontë family—Examinations—Study guides. 2. English fiction—
Women authors—Examinations—Study guides. 3. English fiction—
19th century—Examinations—Study guides.
I. Bloom, Harold. II. Series.
PR4168.B757   1999
823'.809—dc21
99-31887
CIP

Chelsea House Publishers
1974 Sproul Road, Suite 400
Broomall, PA 19008-0914

The Chelsea House World Wide Website address is
http://www.chelseahouse.com

Contributing Editor: Tenley Williams

Contents

User's Guide

This volume is designed to present biographical, critical, and bibliographical information on the playwright's best-known or most important works. Following Harold Bloom's editor's note and introduction are a detailed biography of the author, discussing major life events and important literary accomplishments. A plot summary of each play follows, tracing significant themes, patterns, and motifs in the work.

A selection of critical extracts, derived from previously published material from leading critics, analyzes aspects of each play. The extracts consist of statements from the author, if available, early reviews of the work, and later evaluations up to the present. A bibliography of the author's writings (including a complete list of all works written, cowritten, edited, and translated), a list of additional books and articles on the author and his or her work, and an index of themes and ideas in the author's writings conclude the volume.

∼

Harold Bloom is Sterling Professor of the Humanities at Yale University and Henry W. and Albert A. Berg Professor of English at the New York University Graduate School. He is the author of over 20 books and the editor of more than 30 anthologies of literary criticism.

Professor Bloom's works include *Shelley's Mythmaking* (1959), *The Visionary Company* (1961), *Blake's Apocalypse* (1963), *Yeats* (1970), *A Map of Misreading* (1975), *Kabbalah and Criticism* (1975), and *Agon: Toward a Theory of Revisionism* (1982). *The Anxiety of Influence* (1973) sets forth Professor Bloom's provocative theory of the literary relationships between the great writers and their predecessors. His most recent books include *The American Religion* (1992), *The Western Canon* (1994), *Omens of Millennium: The Gnosis of Angels, Dreams, and Resurrection* (1996), and *Shakespeare: The Invention of the Human* (1998), a finalist for the 1998 National Book Award.

Professor Bloom earned his Ph.D. from Yale University in 1955 and has served on the Yale faculty since then. He is a 1985 MacArthur Foundation Award recipient, served as the Charles Eliot Norton Professor of Poetry at Harvard University in 1987–88, and has received honorary degrees from the universities of Rome and Bologna. In 1999, Professor Bloom received the prestigious American Academy of Arts and Letters Gold Medal for Criticism.

Currently, Harold Bloom is the editor of numerous Chelsea House volumes of literary criticism, including the series BLOOM'S NOTES, BLOOM'S MAJOR SHORT STORY WRITERS, BLOOM'S MAJOR POETS, MAJOR LITERARY CHARACTERS, MODERN CRITICAL VIEWS, MODERN CRITICAL INTERPRETATIONS, and WOMEN WRITERS OF ENGLISH AND THEIR WORKS.

Editor's Note

As there are more than thirty Critical Views excerpted in this short volume, I will confine myself here to a few remarks on those I myself find particularly persuasive.

On Charlotte Brontë's admirable *Villette*, there are useful insights provided by Robert B. Heilman and Carol T. Christ.

Jane Eyre provokes strong commentaries by Virginia Woolf and John Maynard.

V. S. Pritchett and Sheila Smith seem to me quite illuminating on *Wuthering Heights*.

Introduction

HAROLD BLOOM

A particular mark of Charlotte Brontë's *Jane Eyre* is the author's exuberant aggressiveness toward her readership. She bullies and teases us, not so much because she distrusts her readers (perhaps the males somewhat more) but because she has a Byronic temperament, at least as a writer. Her favorite among her contemporaries was Thackeray, but *Vanity Fair* and *Jane Eyre* take place in different solar systems. George Gordon, Lord Byron died, more-or-less heroically, in the Greek rebellion against the Turks, when the Brontë sisters were still little girls. The Byron legend, and the noble lord's poetry, provided the literary context for the Brontës, and helped them create their private genre of Northern romance that triumphed in Charlotte's *Jane Eyre* and Emily's *Wuthering Heights*.

Charlotte's mature version of Byron is Rochester, the much-battered hero of *Jane Eyre*, though Jane herself is equally Byronic in her sexual intensity and her fierce pride. Poor Rochester, partly maimed and partly blinded, is finally a fit husband for Jane, who even at last accomplishes the Byronic surrogate's religious conversion. The male reader can feel a touch disconcerted by Jane's narrative triumphalism, and yet all readers are glad to yield to Charlotte Brontë's remarkable will-to-power over art and life together.

Wuthering Heights, Emily Brontë's solitary novel, is an even greater work than *Jane Eyre*. Though Charlotte Brontë dismissed Heathcliff as "a mere demon," she deceived herself. Heathcliff is of the company of Byron's Manfred, Captain Ahab in Melville's *Moby-Dick*, and Satan in Milton's *Paradise Lost*: these are the sublime hero-villains who stem ultimately from Shakespeare's Macbeth. Heathcliff has only the one quest: to love Catherine Earnshaw, if "love" is the right word to use. So destructive is Heathcliff's passion that sexual fulfillment seems irrelevant to it, being far short of that total fusion implied by Catherine's: "I *am* Heathcliff."

There are two orders of the real in *Wuthering Heights*, with only a void between them. The social and natural worlds form one, while childhood yearnings, visions, dreams, and even ghosts form the other. This second order of reality can be identified with Emily Brontë's deepest self, a vital spark that goes back before the Creation, and that she regarded as what was best and oldest in her. This spark or demiurgic breath is expressed also in her lyric poems, which are of a very high aesthetic quality.

Moral judgments are sometimes relevant to *Jane Eyre*; they are absurdly out of place in regard to *Wuthering Heights*. The daemonic energies of Heathcliff and the first Catherine simply are off the scale of social or natural energies. Heathcliff and his Catherine live, suffer, and die in a world that is not our own, and yet it beckons to something restless and tormented in us. E. M. Forster, reflecting on these occult lovers, wrote that: "*Wuthering Heights* has no mythology beyond what these two characters provide: no great book is more cut off from the universals of Heaven and Hell." It may be that Emily Brontë, like William Blake, dreamed of a Marriage of Heaven and Hell. Her own preternatural genius can seem a prefiguration of just such a mythic marriage. ❁

Biography of
Charlotte Brontë

Charlotte Brontë was born on April 21, 1816, to Patrick and Maria Brontë in Thornton, Lancashire, England. Patrick Brontë, an Irishman, published several undistinguished volumes of prose and verse and Maria Branwell Brontë, a Cornishwoman, demonstrated some literary ability in letters and an unpublished essay. Brontë supported his family, however, by obtaining the curacy of Haworth parish in 1820. A year later, Maria Brontë died, and an aunt took charge of the house and the children.

In 1824, Charlotte and three of her sisters—the two oldest, Maria and Elizabeth, and the younger Emily—were sent to the Clergy Daughters' School at Cowan Bridge. The harsh treatment they received at the boarding school, depicted as Lowood in *Jane Eyre*, contributed to the untimely death of Maria and Elizabeth. Charlotte and Emily then returned home to their father, their brother, Patrick Branwell, and their younger sister, Anne.

The four close-knit siblings spent their days wandering the surrounding Yorkshire moors and reading and writing voraciously. In 1826 their father brought home a box of wooden soldiers that inspired the children to write chronicles of an imaginary world called the Glasstown Confederacy. Gradually Charlotte, with the help of Branwell, channeled her creative energies into describing adventures in the exotic world Angria, while Emily, with the assistance of Anne, turned to the fantasy world Gondal. While Emily continually revisited Gondal in her poems, Charlotte composed *Farewell to Angria* when she was twenty-three.

When they reached adulthood, all three sisters reluctantly left Haworth for a time to become governesses. Preparing to open a school of their own, in 1842 Charlotte and Emily studied foreign languages at a boarding school in Brussels, Belgium, run by Monsieur and Madame Constantin Héger. In 1843, Charlotte became a teacher at the school but suffered from an impossible love for her married employer; the painful situation influenced her later writing.

Charlotte returned home in 1844, and by 1845 the whole family was reunited. Unable to launch their school, the sisters were distracted by domestic troubles; the Reverend Brontë was becoming older and weaker, and the once-talented Branwell was turning to alcohol and opium. However, the Brontë women remained undaunted in their literary ambitions. In 1846, Charlotte convinced Emily and Anne to join her in publishing the pseudonymous *Poems by Currer, Ellis, and Acton Bell.* Though the poetry collection received little notice, the sisters were already completing their first novels.

By 1847, the budding novelists realized mixed results with their works. Emily's *Wuthering Heights* and Anne's *Agnes Grey* were published, while Charlotte's *The Professor,* a rather lackluster account of a Brussels teacher and his marriage, was rejected. Charlotte overcame the disappointment with her next novel, *Jane Eyre,* published in 1847. The novel, a compelling story of a plain, independent governess who finds love under melodramatic circumstances, immediately earned acclaim. In contrast, her sisters' works did not attract much attention during their lifetime. Anne tried again in 1848, with the novel *The Tenant of Wildfell Hall.* When rumors circulated that *Tenant* was actually written by the best-selling author of *Jane Eyre,* Currer Bell (Charlotte's pseudonym), the sisters finally discarded their pseudonyms.

The family's enjoyment of its success was tragically brought to a halt in 1848. After the dissipated Branwell died in September, Emily and Anne caught consumption (tuberculosis); Emily succumbed in December and Anne in May 1849. Battling ill health herself, Charlotte was left alone at Haworth to care for her aging father.

In her final years, Charlotte persevered in her writing. *Shirley,* a novel concerning a small country parish, was published in 1849. During this time, Charlotte occasionally sought relief from her depressing circumstances by traveling to London, where she socialized with other prominent writers, including William Makepeace Thackeray. While visiting friends in northern England in 1850, she was introduced to the novelist Elizabeth Gaskell, who became her first biographer in 1857. Brontë's last novel, *Villette*—the story of an orphan who encounters love while making her own way as a teacher in Belgium—was published in 1853. A year later, she finally accepted Haworth curate Arthur Nicholls's proposal, and the two were married on June 19.

Charlotte Brontë died from pregnancy toxemia on March 31, 1855. *The Professor* (1857) and *Emma*, the fragment of a novel, were published posthumously, and interest in her earlier works continues unabated to this day. ❁

Plot Summary of
Villette

In this novel the theme of surveillance, of watching, helps to structure the story told by Lucy Snowe, poor, plain, and friendless, who leaves England after the death of her employer to teach at a girls' school in the town of Villette, Belgium. In **chapter one** Lucy, the protagonist and narrator, resides in England at the home of her godmother, Mrs. Bretton. We meet Paulina (Polly) Home (**chapters two** and **three**), a distant relation of the late Dr. Bretton. Polly, a serious, unhappy six-year-old who misses her father, becomes attached to Mrs. Bretton's son Graham, "a handsome, faithless-looking youth of sixteen." The childish affection Polly feels for Graham foreshadows the attachment he will feel toward her, years later.

A few weeks after Paulina's departure to join her father "on the Continent," Lucy describes her life of the next eight years as one in which, "like many women and girls," she is "as a bark slumbering through halcyon weather" (**chapter four**). What happens next remains unrevealed. Events have left her as if shipwrecked and isolated, having long ago lost touch with the Bretton family. She is invited to the home of Miss Marchmont, an old rich woman who hires her as a companion. "Two hot, close rooms thus became my world," she observes, "and a crippled old woman, my mistress, my friend, my all." Lucy enjoys the chance to study "the originality of [Miss Marchmont's] character." The real and the imaginary collide here, as they often do in this novel, when the wailing wind seems to Lucy "almost articulate to the ear" one evening. She recalls, "Three times in the course of my life, events had taught me that these strange accents in the storm . . . denote a coming state of the atmosphere unpropitious to life."

After Miss Marchmont's death (**chapter five**), Lucy assesses her possibilities and responds to an inner voice which commands her, "Leave this wilderness . . . and go out hence." To London, she thinks, and adventure. From London, she sails to France, aboard *The Vivid*, where she meets seventeen-year-old Ginevra Fanshawe who is en route to Madame Beck's school in Villette. She urges Lucy to apply there as a teacher (**chapter six**). "And Madame did engage me that very night," Lucy recalls, "—by God's blessing I was spared the necessity of passing forth again into the lonesome, dreary, hostile street." (**chapter seven**). Madame, capable and unscrupulous, "rules by espionage . . . [with] her staff of spies." The observer observed, she cannot escape Lucy's kindly (and shrewd) scrutiny. Lucy's teaching talent does not escape Madame Beck's surveillance. Exiting a class one day (**chapter eight**) Lucy finds that the woman "had been listening and peeping through a spy-hole the whole time. . . . From that day I ceased to be nursery-governess, and became English teacher. [She] raised my salary; but she got thrice the work out of me she had extracted from Mr. Wilson, at half the expense."

Ginevra Fanshawe is both remarkably beautiful and remarkably selfish. She is in love with a mysterious suitor she calls "Isidore." She comments to Lucy that, although he is neither "very pretty" nor wealthy, his ardent love for her leaves her "well amused" (**chapter nine**). Lucy is appalled when she discovers that the extravagant clothing and jewels Ginevra has recently acquired come from Mr. Isidore. She tells her to send the goods back: "It stands to reason that by accepting his presents you give him to understand he will one day receive an equivalent, in your regard. . . ." "But he won't," Ginevra replies, "he has his equivalent now, in the pleasure of seeing me wear them—quite enough for him: he is only bourgeois." Such is the tone of all Ginevra's attachments, yet she and Lucy, student and teacher, become friends

In **chapters ten** through **twelve** Lucy observes the domestic scene at Madame Beck's residence. Madame herself "was a most consistent character; forbearing with all the world, and tender to no part of it. Her own children drew her into no deviation from the even tenor of her stoic calm." A young English doctor comes to care for one of Madame's children and Lucy finds herself unexpectedly attracted to him: "Often, while waiting for Madame, he would muse . . . like a man who thinks himself alone. I, meantime, was free to puzzle over his countenance and wonder what could be the meaning of that peculiar interest and attachment—all mixed up with doubt and strangeness, and inexplicably ruled by some presiding spell—which wedded him to this demi-convent, secluded in the built-up core of a capital. He, I believe, never remembered that I had eyes in my head; much less a brain behind them (**chapter ten**)." By **chapter eleven** Lucy has become an unwitting accomplice in concealing from Madame a love affair that seems to involve Dr. John. In the darkness of the garden one night, Lucy intercepts what may be a billet-doux and Madame, "finely accomplished as she was in the art of surveillance," seems to sense Lucy's involvement, like a "foolish fly," in this web of "things extraordinary transpiring on her premises (**chapter twelve**)."

At the school's summer *fete*, a play being the "main point" of the festivities, Ginevra plays a prominent role directed by the professor of literature at the school, M. Paul Emmanuel, "a harsh apparition"—and an irritable one, reminiscent, in some sense, of *Jane Eyre*'s Rochester. Locked in the attic by M. Emmanuel to learn her lines, Lucy discovers her own acting powers. Comfortable on the stage among the students and teachers, she plays "lover" to Ginevra who, she notices, gazes into the audience at Dr. John. She cannot read "the language" of the look he returns (**chapter fourteen**). After the *fete*, and the return to studies and school examinations, Lucy remains at the school when most have left on vacation, in the company of "a servant, and a poor deformed and imbecile pupil . . . [whose] mind, like her body, was warped; its propensity was to evil . . . [that] made constant vigilance indispensable (**chapter fifteen**)." Juxtaposed with this scene is an "avenging dream" Lucy believes rooted in her growing illusion of Ginevra as a sort of heroine of "True Love." The next day Lucy, a Protestant, seeks spiritual comfort from a Catholic priest. The encounter, while it does not make her a convert to the faith, is notable for its depiction of the search for meaning and personal usefulness that Brontë also treats in *Jane Eyre*. Here, Lucy Snowe comments that, with his "honest, popish superstition," the kindly priest might have "kindled" in her "the zeal of good works." "I might just now," she speculates, "instead of writing this heretic narrative, be counting my beads in the cell of a certain Carmelite convent [in] Villette." The next day Lucy, weak and ill, faints, then awakens into what she thinks is another dream, at the beginning of Volume Two.

Lucy's surroundings, in **chapter sixteen,** suggest to her that she is back in the home of Mrs. Bretton, in England. Gradually, she discovers that she is in the home of Dr. John—Mr. Graham Bretton—and his mother, Mrs. Bretton, Lucy's godmother, where she had been brought after her collapse. Reunited with this family, Lucy will become deeply attached to the young doctor. By the close of **chapter nineteen** Lucy's friendship with Graham is strong, but his affection for Ginevra is foremost in his own mind. Lucy thinks that she has underestimated the clarity of his view of Miss Fanshawe.

She believes that he does indeed know her weaknesses of character. Lucy and Graham attend a formal affair at which Graham, in casual conversation, reveals his predisposition to such infatuation (**chapter twenty**): When Lucy chides him for his gaze toward a cool and "magnetic" beauty, he responds, "[H]ow do you know that the spectacle of her grand insensibility might not with me be the strongest stimulus to homage? The sting of desperation is, I think, a wonderful irritant to my emotions: but . . . you know nothing of that." Lucy is, as always, ruthlessly self-effacing. Of her surprise at catching her reflection in a mirror, she notes, "I enjoyed the 'giftie' of seeing myself as others see me. . . . I ought to be thankful: it might have been worse."

Lucy attends a concert in the company of the Brettons (**chapter twenty**). Ginevra, flighty, flirtatious, and self-absorbed as ever angers Graham by her indifference to him and her appearance with a new male friend. He confides his irritation to Lucy, who, for her part, has angered M. Paul Emmanuel who, she admits, "had penetrated my thought and read my wish to shun him." Lucy regrets that the "calm and modest hope" of her deep friendship with Graham is not sufficient comfort to either of them.

At the close of **chapter twenty-five** Graham, spending the evening with Mrs. Bretton, Mr. Home, Paulina, and Lucy, is observed by Lucy to follow "with his eye the gilded glance of Paulina's thimble, as if it had been some bright moth on the wing, or the golden head of some darting little yellow serpent." Lucy, as always, represses her own feelings for Graham. In **chapter twenty-seven** Graham banters with Lucy: "I believe if you had been a boy, Lucy, instead of a girl—my mother's godson instead of her goddaughter—we should have been good friends: our opinions would have melted into each other." Lucy, trying to "keep down the unreasonable pain" his words cause her, wonders if, had she possessed "the additional advantages of wealth and station," his feelings toward her would be different.

But Lucy feels no resentment. Instead, she attaches her affections to the waspish, despotic, but good-hearted professor M. Paul Emmanuel, Mme. Beck's cousin (volume three, **chapter twenty-eight**). Throughout the story, Lucy struggles to achieve emotional and intellectual strength and independence. When Paul challenges her to intellectual ambition she concludes, "Whatever my powers—feminine or the contrary—God had given them, and I felt resolute to be ashamed of no faculty of His bestowal (**chapter thirty**)." When Paul is called away on business to the West Indies, Lucy is left in charge of her own school. At the novel's close the reader is left to decide whether Paul returns to marry Lucy or is drowned on the trip home.

Villette is not, as might have been expected, a Bildungsroman, a novel of personal development. Lucy does not develop or change in her relations with the society around her; she remains "guiltless of that curse, an overheated imagination." Lucy does establish herself, however, as an adventurous and strong-willed heroine much like her fictional predecessor, Jane Eyre. ✿

List of Characters in
Villette

Lucy Snowe seems in many ways a fulfillment of the character of Jane Eyre. Plain-featured, with neither family nor fortune, she is spurred into action by events not under her control. Her stance toward life is that of an observer of other people's actions and behavior. By this she intends to remain detached, hidden from emotional risk. For awhile, she is able to accomplish this end, first as nurse and companion to the elderly Mrs. Marchmont, then at the girls' school in Villette where she is engaged to teach. Through her encounters in love, first for John Graham Bretton, then with M. Paul Emmanuel, whom she comes to prefer "before all humanity," Lucy becomes Charlotte Brontë's most independent and passionate nineteenth-century heroine.

Madame Beck is the headmistress of the girls' school in Villette, Belgium, who hires Lucy as a teacher. She is "a very great and very capable woman . . . [who] should have been the leader of a turbulent legislative assembly." And, she is "[w]ise, firm, faithless; secret, crafty, passionless; watchful and inscrutable; acute and insenate—withal perfectly decorous—what more could be desired?" She, too, is an observer of people: Lucy notes that "'Surveillance,' 'espionage'—these were her watchwords."

John (Graham) Bretton is the son of Lucy's godmother, Mrs. Bretton. He is the doctor at Madame Beck's school. Lucy falls in love with him, but he knows her only as a friend, preferring, instead, the likes of women such as Ginevra Fanshawe. He and Lucy become friends and he confides to her the tribulations of his infatuation with Ginevra Fanshawe. She watches as his love for Paulina Home replaces this frivolous attraction, and takes great pleasure from the knowledge of their happiness.

Ginevra Fanshawe is a student at Madame Beck's school and a pupil of Lucy's. Vain and frivolous, she is also beautiful and charming. Besides music, singing, and dancing, she is interested only in money, of which she never has enough to satisfy her expensive tastes. Graham becomes infatuated with Ginevra and confides his frustrations about her to Lucy.

Paulina Home is the daughter of a distant relation of the Brettons. From early childhood she has loved Graham. At last, after he has detached his affections from Ginevra, Graham falls in love with Paulina. Lucy tells Paulina, "Providence has protected and cultured you, not only for your own sake, but I believe for Graham's. His star, too, was fortunate: to develop fully the best of his nature, a companion like you was needed: there you are, ready. You must be united."

M. Paul Emmanuel is Madame Beck's cousin and an unromantic hero far removed from the Byronic intensity of *Jane Eyre*'s Edward Rochester. A teacher at the girls' school, M. Emmanuel is, like Lucy, an observer of people. Lucy remarks, "It was very much his habit to wear eyes before, behind, and on each side of him." His directness of speech and honest affection for her eventually charm Lucy, and she agrees to marry him on his return from a business trip to the West Indies. Before sailing, he leaves Lucy the headmistress of her own school. At the end of the story Lucy awaits his return, disturbed by an intense storm that may presage some unknown calamity. We never know if he arrives. ❀

Critical Views on
Villette

[Harriet Martineau (1802–1876) was a prolific author
whose books include the novels *The Peasant and the Prince,
Deerbrook, The Hour and the Man,* and *Dawn Island,* and
the nonfiction works *Retrospect of Western Travel, Society
in America, How to Observe Morals and Manners,* and
Household Education. In this extract, she praises *Villette,* yet
notes that it is inferior to *Jane Eyre.*]

Everything written by "Currer Bell" is remarkable. She can touch
nothing without leaving on it the stamp of originality. Of her three
books, this is perhaps the strangest, the most astonishing, though
not the best. The sustained ability is perhaps greater in *Villette*
than in its two predecessors, there being no intervals of weakness,
except in the form of a few passages, chiefly episodical, of over-
wrought writing, which, though evidently a sincere endeavour to
express real feeling, are not felt to be congenial, or very intelli-
gible, in the midst of so much that is strong and clear. In regard
to interest, we think that this book will be pronounced inferior
to *Jane Eyre* and superior to *Shirley.* In point of construction it is
superior to both; and this is a vast gain and a great encouragement to hope for future benefits from the same hand which shall
surpass any yet given. The whole three volumes are crowded with
beauties—with the good things for which we look to the clear
sight, deep feeling and singular, though not extensive, experience
of life which we associate with the name of "Currer Bell". But
under all, through all, over all, is felt a drawback, of which we were
anxious before, but which is terribly aggravated here—the book
is almost intolerably painful. We are wont to say, when we read
narratives which are made up of the external woes of life, such as
may and do happen every day, but are never congregated in one
experience—that the author has no right to make readers so miserable. We do not know whether the right will be admitted in the
present case, on the ground of the woes not being external; but
certainly we ourselves have felt inclined to rebel against the pain,

and, perhaps on account of protraction, are disposed to deny its necessity and truth. With all her objectivity, "Currer Bell" here afflicts us with an amount of subjective misery which we may fairly remonstrate against; and she allows us no respite—even while treating us with humour, with charming description and the presence of those whom she herself regards as the good and gay. In truth, there is scarcely anybody that is good—serenely and cheerfully good, and the gaiety has pain in it. An atmosphere of pain hangs about the whole, forbidding that repose which we hold to be essential to the true presentment of any large portion of life and experience. In this pervading pain, the book reminds us of Balzac; and so it does in the prevalence of one tendency, or one idea, throughout the whole conception and action. All the female characters, in all their thoughts and lives, are full of one thing, or are regarded by the reader in the light of that one thought—love. It begins with the child of six years old, at the opening—a charming picture—and it closes with it at the last page; and, so dominant is this idea—so incessant is the writer's tendency to describe the need of being loved, that the heroine, who tells her own story, leaves the reader at last under the uncomfortable impression of her having either entertained a double love, or allowed one to supercede another without notification of the transition. It is not thus in real life. There are substantial, heartfelt interests for women of all ages, and under ordinary circumstances, quite apart from love: there is an absence of introspection, an unconsciousness, a repose in women's lives—unless under peculiarly unfortunate circumstances—of which we find no admission in this book; and to the absence of it, may be attributed some of the criticism which the book will meet from readers who are not prudes, but whose reason and taste will reject the assumption that events and characters are to be regarded through the medium of one passion only.

And here ends all demur. We have thought it right to indicate clearly the two faults in the book, which it is scarcely probable that anyone will deny. Abstractions made of these, all else is power, skill and interest. The freshness will be complete to readers who know none but English novels. Those who are familiar with Balzac may be reminded, by the sharp distinction of the pictured life, place, and circumstance, of some of the best of his tales: but there is nothing borrowed; nothing that we might not as well have had if

"Currer Bell" had never read a line of Balzac—which may very likely be the case. As far as we know, the life of a foreign *pension* (Belgian, evidently) and of a third-rate capital, with its half provincial population and proceedings, is new in purely English literature; and most lifelike and spirited it is. The humour which peeps out in the names—the court of Labassecour, with its heir-apparent, the Duc of Dindoneau—the Professors Boissec and Rochemorte—and so forth—is felt throughout, though there is not a touch of lightheartedness from end to end. The presence of the heroine in that capital and *pension* is strangely managed; and so is the gathering of her British friends around her there; but, that strangeness surmounted, the picture of their lives is admirable. The reader must go to the book for it; for it fills two volumes and a half out of the three. The heroine, Lucy Snowe, tells her own story. Every reader of *Jane Eyre* will be glad to see the autobiographical form returned to. Lucy may be thought a younger, feebler sister of Jane. There is just enough resemblance for that—but she has not Jane's charm of mental and moral health, and consequent repose. She is in a state of chronic nervous fever for the most part; is usually silent and suffering; when she speaks, speaks in enigmas or in raillery, and now and then breaks out under the torture of passion; but she acts admirably—with readiness, sense, conscience and kindliness. Still we do not wonder that she loved more than she was beloved, and the love at last would be surprising enough, if love could ever be so. Perhaps Pauline and her father are the best-drawn characters in the book, where all are more or less admirably delineated. We are not aware that there is one failure.

A striking peculiarity comes out in the third volume, striking from one so large and liberal, so removed from ordinary social prejudices as we have been accustomed to think "Currer Bell". She goes out of her way to express a passionate hatred of Romanism. It is not the calm disapproval of a ritual religion, such as we should have expected from her, ensuing upon a presentment of her own better faith. The religion she envokes is itself but a dark and doubtful refuge from the pain which impels the invocation; while the Catholicism on which she enlarges is even virulently reprobated. We do not exactly see the moral necessity for this (there is no artistical necessity) and we are rather sorry for it, occurring as it does at a time when catholics and protestants hate each other quite sufficiently; and in a mode which will not effect conversion. A better advocacy of protestantism would have been to show that it can give rest to the weary and heavy laden; whereas it seems to yield no comfort in return for every variety of sorrowful invocation.

—Harriet Martineau, Review in the *Daily News* (3 February 1853). Reprinted in *The New Moulton's Library*, vol. 8, ed. Harold Bloom (New York: Chelsea House Publishers, 1988): pp. 4484–4485.

⊗

GEORGE HENRY LEWES ON THE MORAL OF THE NOVEL

[George Henry Lewes (1817–1878) was an author, playwright, and critic whose works include *The Noble Heart* (a play), *Ranthorpe, Female Characters of Goethe, On Actors and the Art of Acting,* and *Problems of Life and Mind.* In this extract, Lewes discusses the power of *Villette.*]

There is a moral too in *Villette,* or rather many morals, but not so distinctly a *morale en action.* It is a work of astonishing power and passion. From its pages there issues an influence of truth as healthful as a mountain breeze. Contempt of conventions in all things, in style, in thought, even in the art of story-telling, here visibly springs from the independent originality of a strong mind nurtured in solitude. As a novel, in the ordinary sense of the word, *Villette* has few claims; as a *book,* it is one which, having read, you will not easily forget. It is quite true that the episode of Miss Marchmont, early in the first volume, is unnecessary, having no obvious connexion with the plot or the character; but with what wonderful imagination is it painted! Where shall we find such writing as in that description of her last night, wherein the memories of bygone years come trooping in upon her with a vividness partaking of the last energy of life? It is true also that the visit to London is unnecessary, and has many unreal details. Much of the book seems to be brought in merely that the writer may express something which is in her mind; but at any rate she *has* something in her mind, and expresses it as no other can. ⟨. . .⟩

In this world, as Goethe tells us, "there are so few voices, and so many echoes;" there are so few books, and so many volumes—so few persons thinking and speaking for themselves, so many reverberating vague noises of others. Among the few stands *Villette*. In it we read the actual thoughts and feelings of a strong, struggling soul; we hear the cry of pain from one who has loved passionately, and who has sorrowed sorely. Indeed, no more distinct characteristic of Currer Bell's genius can be named, than the depth of her capacity for all passionate emotions.

> —George Herbert Lewes, "*Ruth* and *Villette*," *Westminster Review* (April 1853): pp. 485–490.

⊚

CATHERINE M. SEDGWICK ON THE BYRONIC INTENSITY OF THE NOVEL

[Catharine Maria Sedgwick (1789–1867) was the author of *The Boy of Mount Rhigi, Hope Leslie, or, Early Times in the Massachusetts,* and an autobiography, *The Power of Her Sympathy.* Here, Sedgwick praises Brontë's intensity.]

Have you all read *Villette?* and do you not admire the book, and own it as one of the great books of the time? I confess that I have seldom been more impressed with the genius of the writer, and seldom less drawn to her personally. She has nerves of such delicate fineness of edge that the least touch turns them, or she has had an exasperating experience. Whether she calls herself Jane Eyre, or Lucy Snowe, it does not matter—it is Miss Brontë. She has the intensity of Byron—of our own Fanny Kemble. She unconsciously infuses herself into her heroine. It is an egotism whose fires are fed by the inferior vitality of others; and how well she conceives others! how she daguerrotypes them!

> —Catharine M. Sedgwick, Letter to Dr. Dewey (April 1853), cited in Mary E. Dewey, *Life and Letters of Catharine M. Sedgwick* (1871): p. 349.

⊚

MARGARET OLIPHANT ON THE NOVEL'S SIMILARITIES TO *Jane Eyre*

[Margaret Oliphant (1828–1897) was the author of *The Literary History of England* and *The Makers of Florence: Dante, Giotto, Savonarola, and Their City*. In this extract from her important work *The Victorian Age of English Literature*, she compares *Villette* to *Jane Eyre*.]

The third of Miss Brontë's works, *Villette*, published 1853, returned in a great measure to the atmosphere of *Jane Eyre*, the scene being chiefly laid in Brussels, and in a school there; and the real hero—after one or two failures—being found in the person of a French master, the fiery, vivacious, undignified and altogether delightful M. Paul Emmanuel, who plays upon the heroine's heart and nerves something after the manner of Rochester, but who is so absolutely real in his fantastic peculiarities and admirable, tender, manly character, that the pranks he plays and the confusion he produces are all forgiven him. Lucy Snowe, the heroine, the cool little proper Englishwoman with the well-concealed volcano under her primness, is by no means so captivating as Jane Eyre, but every detail is so astonishingly true to life, and the force and vigour of the romance—occasionally reaching to fever-heat, and all the more startling from its contrast with the cold white Brussels house, the school atmosphere, and the chill exterior of Miss Snowe—so absorbing, that the book made a still greater impression than *Jane Eyre*, and the ultimate fate of M. Paul, left uncertain at the conclusion, was debated in a hundred circles with greater vehemence than many a national problem.

—Margaret Oliphant, *The Victorian Age of English Literature*, vol. 1 (1892): pp. 307–308.

༼༽

ROBERT B. HEILMAN ON THE MOON AS SYMBOL IN THE NOVEL

[In this essay, originally printed in *Nineteenth-Century Fiction*, Robert B. Heilman explains how Charlotte Brontë uses moon imagery throughout *Villette*.]

In *Villette*, as in *Jane Eyre*, the moon comes into its sharpest dramatic role late in the story. But it obsesses Charlotte enough to keep sliding into earlier scenes: Lucy looks at sleeping Polly Home "by the fitful gleam of moonlight," walks on a European street "by a fitful gleam of moonlight," or gazes at "the polar splendour of the new-year moon—an orb white as a world of ice." In this last, the pictoral fact betrays an odd quiver of aesthetic life, as it does, too, when Miss Marchmont tells of her lover's death: "I see the moon of a calm winter night float full, clear, and cold, over the inky mass of shrubbery, and the silvered turf of my grounds": her lover is thrown from his horse, and she asks, "How could I name that thing in the moonlight before me?"

Gradually we become aware that in some vague way that Charlotte has not defined for herself the moon the stands for something. This is how Lucy puts her envy of the gay Ginevra Fanshawe: "I too felt those autumn suns and saw those harvest moons, and I almost wished to be covered in with earth and turf, deep out of their influence; for I could not live in their light, nor make them comrades, nor yield them affection." What is significant here is that the sun (the only time it appears in a serious treatment of feeling) and the moon could be felt as "comrades" by and could exert "influence" on a human being. This power to influence is more strongly implied in a later reflection of Lucy's:

> Where, indeed, does the moon not look well? What is the scene, confined or expansive, which her orb does not hallow? Rosy or fiery, she mounted . . . while we watched her flushed ascent, she cleared to gold, and . . . floated up stainless into a now calm sky. Did moonlight soften or sadden Dr. Bretton? Did it touch him with romance?

Such passages prepare us for the series of garden scenes involving the "apparitions" that are important in the story. Lucy's first experience of that frightening event takes place—yes, on a moonlight night: "A moon was in the sky, not a full moon, but a young crescent. I saw her through a space in the boughs overhead. She and the stars, visible beside her, were no strangers where all else was strange: my childhood knew them. I had seen that golden sign with the dark globe in its curve leaning on azure, beside an old thorn at the top of an old field, in Old England. . . ." Now this scene is linked with a subsequent crucial garden scene not only by the moonlight but also by Lucy's association of one lighted night scene with another (a habit which shows that Charlotte's lunar sensibility was regular and stable, not casual and erratic). In the later scene Lucy's moral growth is dramatized by her burial of some letters from Graham and by her refusal to flee from the apparition. "At seven o'clock the moon rose," Lucy notes in the documentary style that often finely supports her non-naturalistic episodes, "The air of the night was very still, but dim with a peculiar mist, which changed the moonlight into a luminous haze. In this air, or this mist, there was some quality—electrical, perhaps—which acted in a strange sort upon me. I felt as I had felt a year ago in England— on a night when the aurora borealis was streaming and sweeping round heaven, . . . I felt, not happy, far otherwise, but strong with reinforced strength." The night Lucy refers to is one on which, returning from a visit, she "should have quailed in the absence of moonlight" but for the "moving mystery—the Aurora Borealis": "Some new power it seemed to bring." On that occasion she resolved to got to London, leaving a desolate life behind her, just as now in the garden she is taking steps to leave a life of fear and psychic dependence behind her; each time it is a nocturnal light from the sky that she identifies as the source of the ability to advance: of power and strength.

In the affair with M. Paul that is the major experience in Lucy's life two key scenes are moonlit—one of them in the same old garden. On this night Paul is distressingly cool and detached: ". . . once again he looked at the moon. . . . In a moment he was gone; the moonlit threshold lay pale and shadowless before the closed front-door." Then he gives her a Catholic pamphlet meant to convert her, one of the moves in the sober dramatic treatment of the important religious theme (to be compared, for instance, with Scott's trivializing of it in *Rob Roy*). The moon presides over a still more serious event, this time in another garden: when Paul gives Lucy a school of her own, "Above the poplars, the laurels, the cypresses, and the roses, looked up a moon so lovely and so halcyon, the heart trembled under her smile. . . ." Although the passage is ambiguous, Lucy appears to be addressing the moon when she apostrophizes: "White Angel! let thy light linger; leave its reflection on succeeding clouds; bequeath its cheer to that time which needs a ray in retrospect." (Paul's surname is Emmanuel, and "the assurance of his sleepless interest . . . broke on me like a light from heaven. . . .") The religious implication of the moon imagery is carried further after Paul's proposal: "We walked back to the Rue Fossette by moonlight—such moonlight as fell on Eden—shining through the shades of the Great Garden, and haply gilding a path glorious for a step divine—a Presence nameless." This is the last use of·the moon in Charlotte's last novel, and it is the ultimate reach in her interpretation of the moon—the moon that could hallow a scene, be a comrade, exert an influence, supply strength, echo a great myth, and suggest the presence of the divine. Such a range would not be possible if she were idly summoning and manipulating a cliché.

—Robert B. Heilman, "Charlotte Brontë, Reason, and the Moon," *Nineteenth-Century Fiction* 14, no. 4 (March 1960). Reprinted in *Critical Essays on Charlotte Brontë*, ed. Barbara Timm Gates (Boston: G. K. Hall & Co., 1990): pp. 43–45.

❦

KATE MILLETT ON LUCY SNOWE'S PECULIAR FREEDOM

[Kate Millett is widely regarded as the leading theoretician of the Women's Liberation movement. Her works include *The Prostitution Papers* (1973), *Flying* (1974), and *Sita* (1977). Her first book, *Sexual Politics* (1970), was an attack on feminist oppression and became a rallying point for the feminist movement. In this extract from *Sexual Politics*, Millett calls Lucy's freedom unconventional for the period.]

Villette reads, at times, like another debate between the opposed mentalities of Ruskin and Mill. Lucy is forever alternating between hankering after the sugared hopes of chivalric rescue, and the strenuous realism of Mill's analysis. Brontë demonstrates thereby that she knows what she is about. In her circumstances, Lucy would not be creditable if she were not continuously about to surrender to convention; if she were not by turns silly as well as sensible. So there are many moments when she wishes she were as pretty as Fanshawe, as rich as Polly, occasions when she would happily forgo life itself at a sign that Graham recognizes she was Alice. Born to a situation where she is subject to life-and-death judgments based on artificial standards of beauty, Lucy is subject to a compulsive mirror obsession, whereby each time she looks in the glass she denies her existence—she does not appear in the mirror. One of the most interesting cases of inferiority feelings in literature, Lucy despises her exterior self, and can build an inner being only through self-hatred. Yet living in a culture which takes masochism to be a normal phenomenon in females, and even conditions them to enjoy it, Lucy faces and conquers the attractions Paul's sadism might have held.

Charlotte Brontë has her public censor as well as her private one to deal with. This accounts for the deviousness of her fictional devices, her continual flirtation with the bogs of sentimentality which period feeling mandates she sink in though she be damned if she will. Every Victorian novel is expected to end in a happy marriage; those written by women are required to. Brontë pretends to compromise; convention is appeased by the pasteboard wedding of Paulina Mary and Prince John; cheated in Lucy's escape. .

Escape is all over the book; *Villette* reads like one long meditation on a prison break. Lucy will not marry Paul even after the tyrant has softened. He has been her jailer all through the novel, but the sly and crafty captive in Lucy is bent on evading him anyway. She plays tame, learns all he has to teach her of the secrets of the establishment—its mathematics and Latin and self-confidence. She plays pupil to a man who hates and fears intelligent women and boasts of having caused the only woman teacher whose learning ever challenged his own to lose her job. Lucy endures the baiting about the "natural inferiority of females" with which Paul tortures her all through the lesson, and understands that only the outer surface of his bigotry melts when she proves a good student and thereby flatters his pedagogic vanity. Yet in his simplicity he has been hoodwinked into giving her the keys. The moment they are in her hand, and she has beguiled him into lending her money, renting her a school of her own, and facilitated her daring in slipping from the claws of Madame Beck—she's gone. The keeper turned kind must be eluded anyway; Paul turned lover is drowned.

Lucy is free. Free is alone; given a choice between "love" in its most agreeable contemporary manifestation, and freedom, Lucy chose to retain the individualist humanity she had shored up, even at the expense of sexuality. The sentimental reader is also free to call Lucy "warped," but Charlotte Brontë is hard-minded enough to know that there was no man in Lucy's society with whom she could have lived and still been free. On those occasions when Brontë did marry off her heroines, the happy end is so fraudulent, the marriages so hollow, they read like satire, or cynical tracts against love itself. There was, in Lucy's position, just as in the Brontë's own, no other solution available.

As there is no remedy to sexual politics in marriage, Lucy very logically doesn't marry. But it is also impossible for a Victorian novel to recommend a woman not marry. So Paul suffers a quiet sea burial. Had Brontë's heroine "adjusted" herself to society, compromised, and gone under, we should never have heard from her. Had Brontë herself not grown up in a house of half-mad sisters with a domestic tyrant for father, no "prospects," as marital security was referred to, and with only the confines of governessing and celibacy staring at her from the future, her chief release the group fantasy of "Angria," that collective dream these strange siblings played all their lives, composing stories about a never-never land where women could rule, exercise power, govern the state, declare night and day, death and life—then we would never have heard from Charlotte either. Had that been the case, we might never have known what a resurrected soul wished to tell upon emerging from several long millennia of subordination. Literary criticism of the Brontës has been a long game of masculine prejudice wherein the player either proves they can't write and are hopeless primitives, whereupon the critic sets himself up like a schoolmaster to edit their stuff and point out where they went wrong, or converts them into case histories from the wilds, occasionally prefacing his moves with a few pseudo-sympathetic remarks about the windy house on the moors, or old maidhood, following with an attack on every truth the novels contain, waged by anxious pedants who fear Charlotte might "castrate" them or Emily "unman" them with her passion. There is bitterness and anger in *Villette*—and rightly so. One finds a good deal of it in Richard Wright's *Black Boy*, too. To label it neurotic is to mistake symptom for cause in the hope of protecting oneself from what could be upsetting.

What should surprise us is not Lucy's wry annoyance, but her affection and compassion—even her wit. *Villette* is one of the wittier novels in English and one of the rare witty books in an age which specialized in sentimental comedy. What is most satisfying of all is the astonishing degree of consciousness one finds in the work, the justice of its analysis, the fairness of its observations, the generous degree of self-criticism. Although occasionally flawed with mawkish nonsense (there is a creditable amount of Victorian syrup in *Villette*), it is nevertheless one of the most interesting books of the period and, as an expression of revolutionary sensibility, a work of some importance.

> —Kate Millett, *Sexual Politics* (1969). Reprinted in *Critical Essays on Charlotte Brontë*, ed. Barbara Timm Gates (Boston: G. K. Hall & Co., 1990): pp. 262–264.

⊚

Carol T. Christ on Narrative Styles in the Novel

[Carol T. Christ is the author of *The Finer Optic: The Aesthetic of Particularity in Victorian Poetry* and *Victorian Literature and the Victorian Visual Imagination*. In this extract, she discusses the two narrative styles in *Villette*, and explains that these reflect Brontë's indecision between realistic and imaginative writing.]

In an even more complex way than *Jane Eyre*, *Villette* expresses Charlotte's aesthetic conflict through the conflicts in the personality of its narrator, Lucy Snowe. The novel alternates two narratives styles which speak for its conflicting psychological and aesthetic claims. Lucy describes external events in a meticulously realistic style in which she attempts to suppress entirely the claims of the self. Here, for example, she describes Polly's running out to meet her father:

> Like a bird or a shaft, or any other swift thing, she was gone from the room. How she got the housedoor open I cannot tell; probably it might be ajar; perhaps Warren was in the way and obeyed her behest, which would be impetuous enough. I—watching calmly from the window—saw her, in her black frock and tiny braided apron (to pinafores she had an antipathy), dart half the length of the street . . .

When Lucy turns from external events to describe her solitary meditations, the style of meticulous description gives way to one that is highly rhetorical, inditive, fraught with metaphor, allegory, and allusion, in which the suppressed elements of Lucy's personality struggle to assert themselves. Here, for example, she describes the conflict within her between Reason and Imagination:

> This hag, this Reason, would not let me look up, or smile, or hope: she could not rest unless I were altogether crushed, cowed, broken-in, and broken-down. According to her, I was born only to work for a piece of bread, to await the pains of death, and steadily through all life to despond. Reason might be right; yet no wonder we are glad at times to defy her, to rush from under her rod and give a truant hour to Imagination— *her* soft, bright foe, *our* sweet Help, our divine Hope. We shall and must break bounds at intervals, despite the terrible revenge that awaits our return.

Both modes of narrative are complexly and ambivalently weighted. The style of passive description protects Lucy from the notice she dreads and from the acknowledgment of desire that renders her vulnerable, but her constant self-suppression finally drives her to a nervous breakdown. The imaginative soliloquies contain the book's poetry and energy, but they provoke a craving desire in Lucy that leads to rebellion and frustration.

Villette has no resolution, and its lack of an end suggests Brontë's own inability to resolve her ambivalence. We assume that Paul Emmanuel dies at sea and that Lucy continues to lead a life of emotional privation, but Lucy will not explicitly acknowledge her fate. Brontë thus gives Lucy neither gratified desire nor the necessity of contemplating its frustrations and finally associates herself neither with the romantic nor the realistic principles conflicting in the novel. Yet the complexity of the portrait of the warring impulses in Lucy's temperament suggests Brontë's ability to utilize the energy and to know the outline of her own predicament.

When Lucy describes the performance of the actress Vashti, the judgment she makes expresses the ambivalence toward the imagination in Brontë's art.

> It was a marvelous sight; a mighty revelation.
> It was a spectacle low, horrible, immoral.

Spectacle or revelation, a disease or a gift of the mind—the terms of the conflict show that Brontë herself has not come to a resolution about the principles of her art. She feels on the one hand a moral and pragmatic necessity to repress the imagination which leads her to a Calvinistic realism; she feels on the other hand that imagination gives a kind of joy and intensity the world denies. It might be argued that Brontë's fiction shows the common Victorian ambivalence toward the imagination, and indeed it does. But Brontë's identity as a woman gives that conflict a peculiar significance. As her correspondence with Southey shows, the Victorian conception of woman's place did not allow her autonomous imaginative activity. Charlotte Brontë's complex response to that prohibition—anger, guilt, a self-suppression expressed in a commitment to realism—shapes her attitude toward her own art even as she continues to write. On the one hand, she values imaginative energy as a means of achieving satisfying self-expression; on the other hand, her conviction that the world does not permit women such gratification of desire makes her see that energy as vain, self-indulgent, and delusory. She resorts to a quotidian realism to contain imaginative desire, but she resents her self-imposed discipline. Her novels therefore contain an ambivalence both toward the imagination and toward the containment she often espouses.

Virginia Woolf has written that the woman writer must kill the angel in the house—the socially ordained ideal of feminine self-lessness—in order to achieve the imaginative freedom necessary for the best writing. Her essay reminds us that sexual and imaginative freedom are closely related, that constraints on the one are felt as constraints on the other. Charlotte Brontë never totally killed the angel. She labored under the conviction that women must suppress desires the world will not fulfill even while she valued those desires as the finest elements of her nature. The resulting conflict between her drive for imaginative expression and her conviction of the necessity of imaginative containment consequently gave her art both its limitations and its strengths.

—Carol. T. Christ, "Imaginative Constraint, Feminine Duty, and the Form of Charlotte Brontë's Fiction," *Women's Studies* 6, no. 3 (1979). Reprinted in *Critical Essays on Charlotte Brontë*, ed. Barbara Timm Gates (Boston: G. K. Hall & Co., 1990): pp. 65–67.

BRENDA R. SILVER ON THE USES OF SILENCE AND REVELATION IN THE NOVEL

[Brenda Silver is editor of *Virginia Woolf's Reading Notebooks* and *Rape and Representation*. Here she discusses the ways that Lucy communicates with the reader in *Villette*.]

Early in the second chapter, . . . we read, "I, Lucy Snowe, plead guiltless of that curse, an over-heated and discursive imagination," and we wonder to whom she is speaking and why she talks of herself in this way. The implied listener, depicted as judge and jury, is almost certainly a precursor of the conventional socialized reader before whom Lucy feels it necessary to disclaim the passionate expression of emotion enacted by Polly, even while implicitly admitting its power. Lucy names herself here by emphasizing the cold aspect of her name as well as the light, names herself as the plain, shy, dowerless girl who already perceives that emotions as strong as those displayed by Polly may find no outlet in the world created by her circumstances—and might well hinder her power to survive.

Throughout the first part of the novel, Lucy continues to preserve her self by distancing those emotions that threaten her precarious economic and psychic equilibrium, particularly her feelings for Graham. After a night of suffering, for example, caused by her bitter knowledge that the romance Madame Beck suspects between her and Dr. John does not exist, the "Next day," she tells us, she "was Lucy Snowe again" (chap. 13). A curious cross-over of roles between Polly and Lucy, however, occurs in the one scene where Lucy does act out her love for Graham—the night she loses his letter. "'Oh! they have taken my letter!' cried the grovelling, groping monomaniac": this is Lucy's depiction of herself (chap. 22). The phrase "monomaniac" echoes her previous description of Polly's attachment to her father as "that monomaniac tendency I have ever thought the most unfortunate with which man or woman can be cursed" (chap. 2). The teasing response that Lucy's display of her feelings evokes in Graham makes us feel that her refusal to declare her love to him (she acknowledges it in a variety of ways to herself and her readers) is not neurotic, or evasive, or even mistaken. Graham may guide her in her exploration of her external environment from feelings of kindness or "camaraderie," but he will never perceive her inner life or fulfill her emotional needs. She observes him directly; he, as in the recognition scene in the nursery, sees her in the mirror of his own egotism and therefore fails to see her at all. It is not surprising, then, that she justifies to the reader her decision to conceal her identity from him by saying it would have made little difference had she "come forward and [announced], 'This is Lucy Snowe!'" (chap. 16).

Lucy's public silence and private dialogue with her reader are deliberate responses to what is perhaps the most potentially destructive aspect of her solitude: the isolation of vision that excludes her from the social discourse necessary for an ontological affirmation of self. However great her emotional self-discipline, Lucy realizes early on the need to acknowledge and share her perceptions of reality in order to continue to be. Thus, she reacts to her observation of Polly at the Bretton tea table by confiding, "Candidly speaking, I thought her a little busy body" (chap.2). The as yet unnamed recipient of this confidence serves as crucial function both in the narrative and in Lucy's development, for no one actually present during that scene would have understood Lucy's rejection of Polly's exaggerated acting of the female role, just as no one at La Terrasse, including Mrs. Bretton, "could conceive" her suffering during the long vacation: "so the half-drowned life-boatman [Lucy] keeps his own counsel, and spins no yarns" (chap. 17). Continually a confidante herself, a mediator who interprets the infant Polly's unspoken need to say goodbye to her cherished Graham and who later smooths the way to their union by speaking for them to Mr. Home, Lucy, in her formative years, has no one to hear her unuttered words, or to speak in her place. The one exception is perhaps Miss Marchmont, who interprets Lucy's lack of words when confronted by an unorthodox question about suffering and salvation not as silence but encouragement (chap. 4). No wonder Lucy loves her, and after her death turns increasingly to the reader to fill the gap. Speak she must, though, for to remain silent would be to become the cretin who makes mouths instead of talking, and whose silence becomes a metaphor for Lucy's own potentially arrested development. To overcome this two-fold silence, Lucy evolves another reader, a nonjudgmental reader, a sharer of the insights that she cannot communicate to those more in tune with the accepted social codes.

When first left on her own, however, after the metaphoric ship-wreck, Lucy's recognition of society's power to render her invisible and mute leads her initially to endow her newly created "reader" with the conventional assumptions about women and novels that she must challenge and change for her own life and tale to be plausible. The irony evident in her first direct address to this reader ("I will permit the reader to picture me . . . as a bark slumbering through halcyon weather . . .") allows her simultaneously to mock those who choose to remain locked within their traditional expectations and to offer them an alternate version of reality that would reflect and validate her existence. This same ironic stance informs Lucy's care to keep the reader abreast of the chronological "story" in her narrative, even as she manipulates the sequence and imagery to reveal a deeper stratum of her psychic life and the true meaning of her tale. "Has the reader forgotten Miss Ginevra Fanshawe?" (chap. 9), she asks after she is well established as a teacher and as a prelude to the introduction of Dr. John. The tinge of sarcasm in her question indicates that the perceptive reader will recognize the priorities implicit in the seemingly discontinuous narrative structure: the need for economic security—the effort of learning French and mastering a strange environment—far outweighed any other considerations in those early days. Later, the question "Does the reader, remembering what was said some pages back, care to ask how I answered [Graham's] letters . . .?" (chap. 23) reminds both the curious reader and herself of her need to keep her emotions in check in the midst of the "new creed . . . a belief in happiness" that she has just described.

—Brenda R. Silver, "The Reflecting Reader in *Villette*," *The Voyage In: Fictions of Female Development*, ed. Elizabeth Abel, Marianne Hirsch, and Elizabeth Langland (Hanover, N.H.: University Press of New England, 1983): pp. 90–111.

[Jerome Beaty is the author of *Misreading Jane Eyre: A Postformalist Paradigm, Middlemarch From Notebook to Novel,* and editor of *The Norton Introduction to Literature.* In this extract, he explains that the character of Lucy is written to correct misreading of *Jane Eyre.*]

Villette and *Jane Eyre* are more than merely comparable; Brontë meant *Villette* to correct what she felt was a common misreading of *Jane Eyre,* a misreading not unknown to us today. If young Jane is right to rebel against injustice and stand up for herself, Brontë would hold that she should nonetheless not be so intemperate and violent; if Jane is admirably proud and self-reliant, she should not ignore the limitations of mortal strength and the need for God, for guidance, prayer, and thanksgiving. But Jane is so attractive that it is difficult for readers to see her flaws as flaws, and Brontë was determined that her new heroine would attract no such unqualified approval. As she writes W. S. Williams:

> As to the character of "Lucy Snowe," my intention from the first was that she should not occupy the pedestal to which "Jane Eyre" was raised by some injudicious admirers.

To put Jane on a pedestal is not only to misread the novel, but to deny what Brontë would consider its cosmological truth, its affirmation of the Providential world order. For it is Providence that, by striking the chestnut tree with lightning out of a clear (dark) blue sky, warns the unheeding and self-contented Jane that Rochester's proposal is suspect; it is Providence that leads her in her wanderings on the moors to Moor's End, the residence of the unknown cousins, the Rivers; it is Providence that permits the repentant Rochester's voice to call her across the void when she begs for a sign.

The cosmography of *Villette* is similarly Providential, thought its young heroine's desires are diametrically opposed to those of Jane. Jane wants "to seek real knowledge of life amidst its perils." Lucy would hide herself away from pain and reality by serving the reclusive Miss Marchmont. Jane is chastened and, to a degree, "domesticated." Lucy's choice is also thwarted:

. . . another decree was written. It seemed I must be stimulated into action. I must be goaded, driven, stung, forced to energy. . . . I had wanted to compromise with Fate: to escape occasional great agonies by submitting to a whole life of privation and small pains. Fate would not be so pacified; nor would Providence sanction this shrinking sloth and cowardly indolence.

Driven into the wide world alone, she is led to the very threshold of M de Vauquer's school:

I had planned nothing: I had not time. Providence said, "Stop here; this is *your* inn." Fate took me in her strong hand; mastered my will: directed my actions: I rang the doorbell. . . . Strangely had I been led since morning—unexpectedly had I been provided for.

Jane thirsts for experience, Lucy shirks it. Jane is chastened for her excessive restlessness and self-reliance; Lucy is spurred to action despite her desire to hide. *Villette* thus makes untenable the narrow and simplistic understanding of Providentialism that might be inferred from reading *Jane Eyre* in isolation. The role of Brontë's Providence is not purely patriarchal, nor does it necessarily reward passivity and social conformity with earthly happiness. Its function is not merely to chasten rebelliousness, to domesticate, as it does for Jane; it also energizes, engages, and socializes, as it does for Lucy, making her more adventurous, making her face reality and the outside world, involving her in life and love—and loss.

There are those who see in that loss—surely M. Paul *is* lost at sea—a denial of the Providential world order of *Jane Eyre*: if Lucy must suffer, if that is her fate no matter what she does, no matter how attentive she is to signs, no matter how moral or devout she is, what is Providence for? The answer in the novel is clear: Despite one's suffering, Providence offers solace, to those who will see, by testifying to the immortality of the soul, affirming the existence of Eden and Heaven. This life, after all, is, in the eyes of God and under the aspect of eternity, exceedingly brief; even three score and ten years of suffering is worthwhile if you are assured of an eternity of bliss.

—Jerome Beaty, Afterword to the Signet Classic edition of *Villette* (New York: Penguin Books, 1987): pp. 479–481.

Plot Summary of
Jane Eyre

The opening chapters of *Jane Eyre* describe Jane's early life at Gateshead with the Reed family, where, as an orphan, she is an unloved outsider and a victim of injustice and betrayal. After a violent altercation with her cousin, John Reed, she is locked in the "red room," where images of confinement and hallucination tell an archetypal story of wrongful and horrifying punishment. In **chapter five**, Jane is sent to Lowood Institution where Maria Temple, the superintendent, becomes a role model of compassion, intelligence, and restraint and encourages Jane's intellectual growth. Like all the women in the novel, she helps Jane to reach maturity and to define a woman's limits and possibilities in nineteenth-century Western society. Helen Burns, an older student, becomes a model of patience and perseverance to Jane. Helen's consuming spirituality is impossible for Jane, but her purity and erudition, together with Miss Temple's kindness and trust, inspire Jane "to pioneer [her] way through every difficulty" (**chapters seven** and **eight**).

After an outbreak of typhus claims the lives of many students, including Helen, Lowood is taken over by more generous benefactors. Jane finishes her education and stays on as a teacher. Miss Temple marries and is "lost" to Jane, but her departure causes Jane to consider a life away from Lowood. She places an ad for a position as governess, and Mrs. Fairfax of Thornfield engages her (**chapters nine** and **ten**). At Thornfield Jane awakes to her new duties with expectations of a "fairer era of life." On a tour of the house she hears a "tragic" and "preternatural" laugh that Mrs. Fairfax attributes to a servant, Grace Poole. The conversation turns at once to Adele Varens, Jane's young pupil, who, with no "marked traits of character," seems primarily a literary device by which Jane may be acceptably brought into proximity with Edward Rochester, the "master" of Thornfield.

"Anybody may blame me who likes," Jane remarks in **chapter twelve,** challenging the reader to criticize her restless desire for more wide-ranging life experiences. In **chapters thirteen** through **fifteen** she and Rochester probe each other's character with considerable rhetorical flair. She considers the intimacy of their conversation and wonders at her "power to amuse him." Jane begins to love Rochester, though she yet admits only that "his presence in the room was more cheering than the brightest fire."

"Goblin-laughter" disturbs Jane's sleep (**chapter fifteen**), and she wonders if the "unnatural sound" is Grace Poole "possessed by a devil." Searching for Mrs. Fairfax Jane sees smoke coming from Rochester's room: She finds him overcome by smoke and unresponsive: She "baptizes" him with all the water she can find. Rochester tells Jane to say nothing of the incident and quickly blames Grace Poole.

Jane considers, with some satisfaction, the character of her relationship with Rochester. She ponders the "pleasure of vexing and soothing him by turns." They are intellectual equals, and she happily anticipates their continued conversation. Her mood changes when Rochester brings to Thornfield the accomplished and "noble"-featured Blanche Ingram and her sisters. Jane chastises herself as a "fool" for having "rejected the real" and "rabidly devoured the ideal." Jane becomes acutely conscious of her love for Rochester when he seems unaware of her presence: "He made me love him without looking at me." At an evening party with the Ingrams, a mysterious gypsy fortune teller appears at the house and is invited to entertain the guests (**chapter eighteen**). The old woman suggests to Jane that she would do well to show more affection to Rochester. Jane is surprised when Rochester reveals himself as the one disguised: She tells him that a stranger named Mason, from the West Indies, has arrived that morning. Rochester, stunned, asks Jane if she would "dare censure" for his sake (**chapter nineteen**).

Awakened that night by the "glorious gaze of the moon upon her," Jane is next startled by a single "savage" cry from the third floor (**chapter twenty**). Rochester, descending from the upper floor with a candle, reassures the guests that a servant has only had a nightmare. He asks Jane's help and brings her to a third-floor room where Mason lies bleeding, attacked by someone now locked in an inner room: Jane thinks it must be Grace Poole. Afterwards Jane and Rochester walk in the garden and he tells her an enigmatic tale of youthful indiscretion and bad judgment that Jane cannot fathom. He sardonically asks her if she will sit up with him the night before he marries Blanche.

In **chapter twenty-one** Jane returns to Gateshead to oversee the dissolution of the Reed family and the death of her aunt—an episode that fulfills her childhood revenge fantasy in the red-room. John Reed has committed suicide after squandering his estate; his mother is dying of a stroke; Georgiana is "very plump" and useless, eventually to marry a dissipated gentleman; and the cold Eliza is leaving for a nunnery. Jane is also in transition: Convinced that Rochester is lost to her, she feels once more "a wanderer on the face of the earth." The passion of childhood resentment has been replaced by a compassion for human weakness and a desire for love and spiritual wholeness.

A "fortnight of dubious calm" follows Jane's return to Thornfield during which Rochester torments her with allusions to his forthcoming wedding. In **chapter twenty-three** he names Jane as his intended bride. At the close of **chapter twenty-four** she observes that Rochester stands "like an eclipse" between her and "every thought of religion." She cannot "see God for His creature: of whom [she] had made an idol."

Jane's disturbing dreams on the nights before her wedding (**chapter twenty-five**) foreshadow disaster. Mason interrupts the ceremony to tell that Rochester already has a wife, Mason's sister, living at Thornfield (**chapter twenty-six**). Rochester takes Jane and the others to the room where Bertha Rochester is confined. She is almost as tall as her husband, "corpulent" and "virile," everything that Jane is not—yet her dark double. Bertha is an extreme of unrestrained physicality and passion, a Victorian female run amok. Her uncontrolled acts are a warning of the dangers to Jane in surrendering herself to physical passion. Jane experiences an epiphany: "a remembrance of God." She must leave Thornfield to preserve her spiritual self. But Rochester asks her to live with him as lover, if not wife. That night, in a dream (**chapter twenty-seven**), the moon advises her: "My daughter, flee temptation." She wakes and answers, "Mother, I will."

Jane flees Thornfield and, after circumstances have left her destitute, she follows a distant light to the cottage at Marsh End where she is taken in by the Rivers family (**chapter twenty-eight**). **Chapters twenty-nine** through **thirty-five** focus upon Jane's sojourn at Marsh End with Diana and Mary, who are about to leave for positions as governesses, and their clergyman brother, St.

John, who plans to devote himself to missionary work. Their father has died and their income is gone. St. John finds Jane a teaching position. Diana remarks that her brother is "inexorable as death" in his vocation and willing to sacrifice all "natural affection." Before leaving on their separate missions the family learns of the death of a distant uncle, their last hope, who has left them no money and thus no reprieve from their scattering.

Jane moves into the little room attached to the schoolhouse where St. John confides to her that he must overcome "a last conflict with human weakness," his love for Rosamond Oliver, the daughter of the school's benefactor (**chapters thirty-one** and **thirty-two**). Jane counsels him against such sacrifice, encouraging him to balance his vocation with the inclinations of his heart—perhaps to work locally. But his "great work" consumes everything.

In **chapter thirty-three** St. John learns Jane's identity and confronts her. He also tells her that the Rivers' dead uncle was the same Mr. Eyre who is related to Jane—and that she has inherited twenty-thousand pounds. Jane divides the inheritance among them, and the family reunites at Marsh End. In such domestic intimacy an intense relationship develops between Jane and St. John that will tempt her to abandon her desire for her own vocation. "By degrees," she notes (**chapter thirty-four**), "[St. John] acquired a certain influence over me that took away my liberty of mind. . . . I fell under a freezing spell."

But all the while, the idea of Rochester—"not a vapor sunshine could dispel"—haunts Jane. His sexuality contrasts St. John's "Greek face" and his marblelike, "experiment" kiss. She writes to Mrs. Fairfax for information about Rochester and, when there is no reply, she gives up hope. When St. John asks her to accompany him to India (**chapter thirty-five**) as his wife Jane sees that such a marriage would be martyrdom to a man who would "scrupulously observe" the "forms of love" without any love at all. She will go, she tells him, as a sister. St. John wears down her resistance by his considerable store of Christian rhetorical weaponry. She asks Heaven for some sign and warns the reader that what happens next may be either telepathy of hysteria: She hears Rochester call her name. With that she has the resolve to dismiss St. John and leave for Thornfield.

Jane arrives to find Thornfield burned out and abandoned (**chapter thirty-six**). An innkeeper tells her a story of a young governess, a lunatic wife, and a thwarted marriage. By a lapse of gin-drinking Grace Poole, Bertha Rochester escaped and set fire to the house and threw herself off the battlements as Rochester tried to save her. He himself was blinded and lost a hand in the disaster. He is at Ferndean, in the care of two servants, where Jane hurries to find him (**chapter thirty-seven**).

"Reader, I married him," Jane famously asserts in **chapter thirty-eight**. Jane and Rochester are equals in this unusual marriage, but a cruel irony undercuts their equality: Mutilation and isolation are necessary to their happiness. Rochester is a Byronic figure made human, and their intense and romantic union is possible only in charmed seclusion. Jane reveals that the events narrated are ten years past, during which time they have had a son and Rochester has regained enough vision to walk without being led.

Jane ends her narrative with the conclusion to the story of St. John Rivers. He is a missionary in India, unmarried, and near death. Jane has "human tears" and "divine joy," certain that his hope for paradise will be realized. For St. John, it is the happiest possible ending. For Jane, an earthly paradise is enough. ❁

List of Characters in
Jane Eyre

Jane Eyre is the narrator and protagonist of the novel, a penniless orphan who eventually realizes her vocation in a marriage of high caste and unusual equality. Without money, known family connections, or beauty, she is educated to become a governess, thereby fulfilling a nineteenth-century convention. But, because of her intelligence, her passionate nature, and, paradoxically, her lack of family claims and restraints, Jane is free to imagine a life of greater experience and intensity in which to enjoy her intellectual gifts. She relies upon her own force of character and will to overcome the lopsided power relations of Victorian society, resisting victimization among the Reed family; self-immolation on the model of Helen Burns; ethical compromise in the romantic love of Edward Rochester; and spiritual self-effacement within St. John Rivers's religious vocation. In a novel permeated with bad weather, pagan and Christian imagery, and considerable physical and psychological stress, Jane Eyre perseveres to achieve a marriage of highly romantic love, intellectual equality, and physical passion.

Edward Rochester is the master of Thornfield, where Jane is employed as a governess when she leaves Lowood Institution. He is a Byronic figure—dark, brooding, volatile, and erotic. Jane observes that, while he is not handsome, his features are somehow harmonious and pleasing to her. He is a lonely and tormented man, though popular and sociable among his upper-class peers. Although of a different class, he is intrigued by Jane's forthright wit and intelligence, and their mutual attraction and regard becomes highly charged, romantic love. Their first wedding ceremony is halted by the disclosure that he has a lunatic wife, but when Jane finally returns to him—after his mutilation and her financial ascent—their physical and spiritual love for each other is undiminished, and they meet each other as equals.

St. John Rivers is Jane's cousin who saves her from death on the heath at Marsh End. He is a clergyman and a Christian zealot who tempts her to bury her desire for a vocation within his own as a missionary in India. He is classically handsome and as cold as a statue in matters of the heart. His beauty and sterility are the opposite of Rochester's rugged and erotic physicality. Jane is drawn to St. John because she recognizes in him her own spiritual longings. She senses that he denies his natural tenderness by an excess of Christian piety and purpose. She almost capitulates to his spiritual intensity, but the lack of physical love finally turns her away from him.

Bertha Rochester is the woman Rochester married in the West Indies as a young man, and who subsequently became mad. Locked in a third-floor room, she laughs preternaturally, disturbing and puzzling Jane until her existence is revealed and Rochester takes Jane to see the violent and wild specter that is his wife. After Jane leaves Thornfield, Bertha starts the fire that destroys the house and mutilates Rochester. She is an example and a confirmation of the dangers of untempered passion and physicality.

Maria Temple is the superintendent of Lowood Institution. Her intelligence, kindness, and gentility guide the lonely Jane into a circumspect and realistic young womanhood. They are friends and become colleagues at the school. When Miss Temple leaves Lowood to be married, Jane feels it as a personal loss.

Helen Burns is a highly intelligent and deeply spiritual student at Lowood, who is a favorite of Maria Temple and of Jane. She counsels Jane against indulging in anger and dwelling upon personal injustice and indignity. She endures the cruelties of illness and the school as if already on her way to an otherworldly paradise. Helen inspires Jane by her strength but saddens her by her self-immolation. She dies of typhus.

Diana and **Mary Rivers,** with their brother, St. John, compose a family for Jane. They are bluestockings, nineteenth-century women who are well read and strong in their ideas and opinions. Jane is happy in their company at Marsh End and happier still to share with them her inheritance from the uncle who, coincidentally, was uncle to them all.

Grace Poole is hired by Rochester to care for Bertha Rochester in the third-floor room. For months, Jane attributes the disturbing laugh she hears to Grace, not suspecting any other possibility. After the fire in Rochester's room, which he tells her is the work of Grace, Jane is confounded by the continued presence of this coarse-featured, gin-drinking enigma.

Adele Varens, the product of Rochester's liaison with a French singer who exchanged her affection for money, is the young child for whom Jane is hired as governess at Thornfield. ❀

Critical Views on
Jane Eyre

VIRGINIA WOOLF ON CHARLOTTE BRONTË AS POET

[Virginia Woolf (1882–1941), aside from being one of the most distinguished British novelists of the twentieth century, was also an astute critic. Her critical work is gathered in several volumes, including *The Common Reader* (1925), *A Room of One's Own* (1929), and *The Moment and Other Essays* (1942). In this extract, Woolf finds *Jane Eyre* representative of a poetic instinct in Charlotte Brontë, in which the natural world symbolizes human emotions.]

Of the hundred years that have passed since Charlotte Brontë was born, she, the centre now of so much legend, devotion, and literature, lived but thirty-nine. It is strange to reflect how different those legends might have been had her life reached the ordinary human span. She might have become, like some of her famous contemporaries, a figure familiarly met with in London and elsewhere, the subject of pictures and anecdotes innumerable, the writer of many novels, of memoirs possibly, removed from us well within the memory of the middle-aged in all the splendour of established fame. She might have been wealthy, she might have been prosperous. But it is not so. When we think of her we have to imagine someone who had no lot in our modern world; we have to cast our minds back to the fifties of the last century, to a remote parsonage upon the wild Yorkshire moors. In that parsonage, and on those moors, unhappy and lonely, in her poverty and her exaltation, she remains for ever.

These circumstances, as they affected her character, may have left their traces on her work. A novelist, we reflect, is bound to build up his structure with much very perishable material which begins by lending it reality and ends by cumbering it with rubbish. As we open *Jane Eyre* once more we cannot stifle the suspicion that we shall find her world of imagination as antiquated, mid-Victorian, and out of date as the parsonage on the moor, a place only to be visited by the curious, only preserved by the pious. So we open *Jane Eyre*; and in two pages every doubt is swept clean from our minds.

> Folds of scarlet drapery shut in my view to the right hand; to the left were the clear panes of glass, protecting, but not separating me from the drear November day. At intervals, while turning over the leaves of my book, I studied the aspect of that winter afternoon. Afar, it offered a pale blank of mist and cloud; near, a scene of wet lawn and storm-beat shrub, with ceaseless rain sweeping away wildly before a long and lamentable blast.

There is nothing there more perishable than the moor itself, or more subject to the sway of fashion than the 'long and lamentable blast'. Nor is this exhilaration short-lived. It rushes us through the entire volume, without giving us time to think, without letting us lift our eyes from the page. So intense is our absorption that if someone moves in the room the movement seems to take place not there but up in Yorkshire. The writer has us by the hand, forces us along her road, makes us see what she sees, never leaves us for a moment or allows us to forget her. At the end we are steeped through and through with genius, the vehemence, the indignation of Charlotte Brontë. Remarkable faces, figures of strong outline and gnarled feature have flashed upon us in passing; but it is through her eyes that we have seen them. Once she is gone we seek for them in vain. Think of Rochester and we have to think of Jane Eyre. Think of the moor, and again there is Jane Eyre. Think of the drawing-room, even, those 'white carpets on which seemed laid brilliant garlands of flowers', that 'pale Parian mantelpiece' with its Bohemia glass of 'ruby red' and the 'general blending of snow and fire'—what is all that except Jane Eyre?

The drawbacks of being Jane Eyre are not far to seek. Always to be a governess and always to be in love is a serious limitation in a world which is full, after all, of people who are neither one nor the other. The characters of a Jane Austen or of a Tolstoy have a million facets compared with these. They live and are complex by means of their effect upon many different people who serve to mirror them in the round. They move hither and thither whether their creators watch them or not, and the world in which they live seems to us an independent world which we can visit, now that they have created it, by ourselves. Thomas Hardy is more akin to Charlotte Brontë in the power of his personality and the narrowness of his vision. But the differences are vast. As we read *Jude the Obscure* we are not rushed to a finish; we brood and ponder and drift away from the text in plethoric trains of thought which build up round the characters an atmosphere of question and suggestion of which they are themselves, as often as not, unconscious. Simple peasants as they are, we are forced to confront them with destinies and questionings of the hugest import, so that often it seems as if the most important characters in a Hardy novel are those which have no names. Of this power, of this speculative curiosity, Charlotte Brontë has no trace. She does not attempt to solve the problems of human life; she is even unaware that such problems exist; all her force, and it is the more tremendous for being constricted, goes into the assertion, 'I love', 'I hate', 'I suffer'. ⟨. . .⟩

In other words, we read Charlotte Brontë not for exquisite observation of character—her characters are vigorous and elementary; not for comedy—hers is grim and crude; not for a philosophic view of life—hers is that of a country parson's daughter; but for her poetry. Probably that is so with all writers who have, as she has, an overpowering personality, so that, as we say in real life, they have only to open the door to make themselves felt. There is in them some untamed ferocity perpetually at war with the accepted order of things which makes them desire to create instantly rather than to observe patiently. This very ardour, rejecting half shades and other minor impediments, wing its way past the daily conduct of ordinary people and allies itself with their more inarticulate passions. It makes them poets, or, if they choose to write in prose, intolerant of its restrictions. Hence it is that both Emily and Charlotte are always invoking the help of nature. They both feel the need of some more powerful symbol of the vast and slumbering passions in human nature than words or actions can convey.

—Virginia Woolf, "*Jane Eyre* and *Wuthering Heights*" (1916). In *Collected Essays*, vol. 1, ed. Leonard Woolf (New York: Harcourt, Brace & World, 1967): pp. 185–188.

RICHARD CHASE ON THE STRUGGLE BETWEEN JANE EYRE AND ROCHESTER

[Richard Chase (1914–1962) wrote a number of critical works including *Herman Melville: A Critical Study* (1949). In this extract, Chase studies the emotional and social conflict between Jane Eyre and Rochester.]

In that somewhat fantastic Gothic-Byronic character Edward Rochester we have Charlotte Brontë's symbolic embodiment of the masculine *élan.* Jane Eyre's feelings toward Rochester are ambivalent. He draws her to him with a strange fascination; yet she is repelled by his animalism and his demonism. She wishes to submit herself to him; yet she cannot. She is nearly enthralled by the "tenderness and passion in every lineament" of his "kindled" face; yet she shrinks from the flashing of his "falcon eye" and from the glamor of his self-proclaimed guilt and his many exploits among women of other countries (in France, Céline; in Italy, Giacinta; in Germany, Clara— "these poor girls" Jane calls them). She cannot permit the proffered intimacies of this man who keeps a mad wife locked up in his attic. And if her moral scruples would allow his embrace, still she could not endure the intensity of his passion. The noble, free companionship of man and woman does not present itself to her as a possibility. She sees only two possible modes of behavior; meek submission or a flirtatious, gently sadistic skirmishing designed to keep her lover at bay. Finally her sense of "duty" compels Jane to run away. The inevitable parting of the lovers had been forecast when the lightning, summoned from the sky by their first declaration of love, had split the garden chestnut tree asunder.

The splitting of the tree, however, may also symbolize two alternate images of Jane Eyre's soul, two possible extremes which, as she believes, her behavior may take. At one extreme is Bertha, Rochester's mad wife; at the other is St. John Rivers, the clergyman cousin whom Jane meets after she flees Rochester and who wants to marry her. Before the story can end, Jane must purge these extreme images of herself. Bertha represents the women who has given herself blindly and uncompromisingly to the principle of sex and intellect. As Fanny E. Ratchford (the expert in the voluminous juvenile romances written by the Brontës) has shown, the character of Bertha was evolved from a certain Lady Zenobia Ellrington, a heroine of Charlotte Brontë's childish fantasy-kingdom of Angria.

Miss Ratchford describes Lady Zenobia thus: She was a "noble woman of strong mind and lofty thought. On the other hand, she is given to fits of rage in which she shrieks like a wild beast and falls upon her victim hand and foot. On one occasion she kicked Lord Charles [a juvenile version of Rochester] down the stairs." Always she is depicted as tall of stature and strong of body. Lord Charles once declared that she could spar on equal terms with her husband, "one of the best boxers on record." She was, furthermore, a learned and intellectual woman, a bluestocking in fact. Like Bertha, she was a Creole and came from a family notorious for mad crimes and passions. May not Bertha, Jane seems to ask herself, be a living example of what happens to the woman who gives herself to the Romantic Hero, who in her insane suffragettism tries herself to play the Hero, to be the fleshly vessel of the *élan*?

We may think that fear drives Jane away from Rochester; *she*, however, says that it is "duty." In St. John Rivers she meets duty incarnate. In a poem Charlotte Brontë had imagined herself as a missionary to the pagans. No "coward love of life," she says, has made "me shrink from the righteous strife." Rivers has given up Rosamond Oliver, a charming and life-loving girl, and wants to marry Jane and take her to India, where he plans to devote himself to missionary work. Plainly, it would be a sexless marriage. Rivers wants a wife to "influence." He is cold, selfish, fanatical—a narrow bigot, who shakes Jane's confidence in "duty." She cannot marry Rivers; she must purge her soul of the image of "duty" as she has of the image of Bertha.

How to resolve the plot? It must be done as Charlotte, the leader of her sisters in all practical matters, was accustomed to do things: by positive action. The universe conspiring against Jane Eyre, like the circumstances which so often conspired against the sisters, must be chastened by an assertion of will, catastrophic if necessary. And so Charlotte sends Rochester's house up in flames and makes him lose his eyesight and his left hand in a vain attempt to save Bertha. Rochester's injuries are, I should think, a symbolic castration. The faculty of vision, the analysts have shown, is often identified in the unconscious with the energy of sex. When Rochester had tried to make love to Jane, she felt a "fiery hand grasp at her vitals"; the hand, then, must be cut off. The universe, not previously amenable to supernatural communication between the parted lovers, now allows them to hear each other though they are leagues apart. It is as if the masterless universe had been subdued by being lopped, blinded, and burned. Jane Eyre now comes into her own. She returns to Rochester. She baits him coyly about her relations with Rivers; he exhibits manly jealousy. They settle dowb to a mild married life; they have a child; Rochester partly, but only partly, regains his eyesight. The tempo and energy of the universe can be quelled, we see, by a patient, practical woman.

—Richard Chase, "The Brontë's, or, Myth Domesticated." In *Forms of Modern Fiction*, ed. William Van O'Connor (Minneapolis: University of Minnesota Press, 1948): pp. 107–109.

☙

Robert Bernard Martin on the Cosmic Scope of Brontë's Imagination

[Robert Bernard Martin is Citizens' Professor of Humanities at the University of Hawaii. He has written biographies of Tennyson (1980), Edward FitzGerald (1985), and Gerard Manley Hopkins (1991). In this extract from his book on Charlotte Brontë's novels, Martin finds the greatness of *Jane Eyre* to rest in the cosmic scope of Brontë's imagination, which takes all of life for its focus.]

'Novelists should never allow themselves to weary of the study of real life,' wrote Charlotte Brontë with sweet reasonableness in *The Professor*. Then, rather less convincingly: 'If they observed this duty conscientiously, they would give us fewer pictures chequered with vivid contrasts of light and shade; they would seldom elevate their heroes and heroines to the heights of rapture—still seldomer sink them to the depths of despair; for if we rarely taste the fulness of joy in this life, we yet more rarely savour the acrid bitterness of hopeless anguish.' In short, such conscientious novelists would not write *Jane Eyre*.

The primary impression of Miss Brontë's first masterpiece is of anguished torment and nearly intolerable happiness. Because she believed that life's joys are few beside its sorrows, ⟨. . .⟩ the reader's strongest recollection is probably of the blinding fierceness of the rebellion of Jane's lonely heart against the loveless tyranny of

Gateshead, the pangs of her physical and emotional hunger at Lowood, the aching frustration of her first love of Rochester, the death-in-life of her discovery that he is already married, the solitary agony of her night on the moor, her merciless grinding under the juggernaut of St. John's ambitious piety. The fitful ecstasy of Jane's joy is made brighter by being thrown in relief against her trials and by the rareness of its visitation: the lyrical garden scene when Rochester pours out his love against a counterpoint of the nightingale's song; the night when he swoops her into his saddle before him like a demon lover enveloping her in his cloak; the muted, autumnal delicacy of their reconciliation at Ferndean, poised between laughter and tears.

The play of Charlotte Brontë's imagination achieves many of its finest effects by lurid contrasts of illumination and shade, by the relentless light of rational day set against the menacing shadows of dead of night ('ever the hour of fatality at Thornfield'), by the juxtaposition of pinafores and supernatural flashes of light, burnt porridge and raging epidemic, schoolroom doldrums and the long, terrible laughter of Grace Poole—or is it the lunatic mirth of Bertha?—housecleaning and a universe shaken by supernatural convulsions: the counterpoise of a world of mundane detail and the world of Gothic imagination. It is a witch's broth of ingredients, but for the first time Charlotte Brontë has the imaginative, comprehensive grasp of her material that manages to fuse its disparate parts into a real unity, one probably owing more to the singleness of her vision than it does to her formal considerations of the problems of structure in the novel. Whether the pattern she achieved was a completely deliberate and rational one, or whether it sprang from somewhere beneath the surface of her consciousness is ultimately unimportant. The heart has its forms, as well as its reasons, that the reason knows nothing of. The novel is improbable in the sense that all cosmic and supernatural action is improbable, even when it seems inevitable. It is larger than life because it is Miss Brontë's vision of the totality of life, of man's relation to his heart, mind, loved ones, and God, and any such vision must necessarily transcend the probable limits of experience of any individual.

—Robert Bernard Martin, *The Accents of Persuasion: Charlotte Brontë's Novels* (New York: Norton, 1966): pp. 57–58.

[Richard Benvenuto is the author of *Emily Brontë* (1982) and *Amy Lowell* (1985). In this extract, Benvenuto asserts that the chief conflict in *Jane Eyre* is in Jane's moral struggle between the state of nature and the state of grace.]

If Jane's conflict had as its base a single personality, the conflict would be resolvable once Jane learned to adjust the relative claims of her reason and her emotions upon her sense of self-identity, and once she learned to use either as a corrective for the exaggerated claims of the other. But nature and grace do not make relative claims upon Jane. They stand for two self-identities, for forces inclusive of her whole being, which is divided so completely that two self-images claim possession of all her human faculties. When Jane defends the moral integrity of the poor, she is not speaking passionately and in defiance of reason, or vice versa. She is emotionally, intellectually, and morally convinced of what she says. And likewise, with her total being, reflectively and feelingly, she revolts from the memory of having had to beg. Not one unitive personality with different parts to it, but two unitive personalities contesting against each other make up her character. There is much to be said for seeing her conflict as critics have generally presented it—not the least of which is that it results in a novel of greater consistency than I am able to find. The portraits of Rochester and St. John speak more directly to a conflict between passion and conscience than perhaps they do to the larger division of nature and grace. But even if it turns out that Rochester and St. John are no more than embodiments of passion and conscience, they cause Jane to define her total being in two ways, to commit herself to two schemes of existence, in each of which there is room for different notions of passionate and rational behavior. A character divided by passion and conscience normally will fluctuate between them as he comes under the temporary sway of each. Though she contradicts herself, Jane does not fluctuate, properly speaking. She makes firm commitments to the life offered by nature and to the life offered by grace.

Jane's commitment to nature occurs when she hears Rochester's voice, just as St. John is about to coerce her into accepting an empty form of marriage. It is a complete endorsement of her own personality, a recognition of her native self as its own absolute norm. Rochester's voice was "no miracle," but the "work of nature. She was roused, and did . . . her best." Nature, in this role, is not an impersonal force or an abstract, external system. The next morning Jane remembers a strange "inward sensation" preceding Rochester's voice. The voice itself had "seemed in *me*—not in the external world." It was "like an inspiration. The wondrous shock of feeling had come like the earthquake which shook the foundations of Paul and Silas's prison; it had opened the doors of the soul's cell and loosed its bands" (original italics). St. John represents duty, suppression, obedience: the behavior and the attitude required by the absolute external morality of grace. He would force Jane to seek acceptance in the terms of the law he serves, with no more room for compromise than he has given himself. These is no meeting the demands of grace halfway. Jane must either go to India as St. John's lawful wife, or not go at all. As Jane's description of it makes clear, Rochester's voice is her voice speaking in the tones of an absolute internal norm—nature, or her individuality. The voice reveals to her the foundations of her being. It is a power like an earthquake, breaking down the prison of religious duty and social code. It is as fundamental as breathing—an inspiration. As her liberation from the false ascendency of St. John, Rochester's voice speaks for Jane's truest life, not merely for her feelings, but for her deepest aspirations, her self-consciousness. There can be no mistake about the intent of the episode. Jane is right to assume the ascendency over St. John, right to leave him, and right to speak for her individual self and unique portion of existence.

But though it is clear that Jane is right to commit herself totally to nature, when St. John would force her into the service of grace, it is not clear how this commitment affects or even relates to her earlier, equally entire commitment to grace, when Rochester asks her to align herself with nature and become his mistress. Jane's return to Rochester raises the question of why she left him, though Jane never acknowledges that it was an error to have left him. Charlotte Brontë does not mean it to appear as such. She sanctions Jane's leaving St. John to return to Rochester, and she sanctions Jane's leaving Rochester and taking the road that leads her to St. John. Jane herself senses that her directions are unclear, but she can express her predicament only through the abstractions, judgment and principle. Just before she hears Rochester's voice, Jane says that she "was almost as hard beset" now as she "had been once before, in a different way, by another. I was a fool both times. To have yielded then would have been an error of principle; to have yielded now would have been an error of judgment." She might have said, almost a fool, since she did not yield to either. Jane's assessment of her dilemma, however, is a more comprehensive one than would be required by a conflict limited to conscience and passion. It is as close as Jane comes to recognizing the totality of the commitments exacted by nature and grace.

The choice between the two amounts to a choice between a relativistic or situational morality and a fixed, universal moral code, between living outside any established religious framework and living as a Christian. Speaking for Christianity and for a moral code handed down through time, St. John asks Jane to continue in the direction she took when she left Rochester, the direction of principle or moral law not subject to individual variation or change. To have yielded would have been an error of judgment, a violation of the thought and moral awareness which she brings to her time. Rochester, on the other hand, makes an explicit appeal to a relativistic ethics and to Jane's innate powers of thought and her right to a self-made moral life. "Is it better," Rochester asks, "to drive a fellow-creature to despair than to transgress a mere human law—no man being injured by the breach?" The "mere human law" is the commandment forbidding adultery and the cultural ban on bigamy. To have yielded would have been an error of principle, against Jane's sense of what is everywhere and eternally right. To put Jane's statement somewhat differently: by opposing Rochester, she yielded to a sense of her moral life as properly under the control and guidance of others, authorities with greater responsibility than her own; by opposing St. John, she yielded to a sense of her moral life as properly under her control and shaping, and she accepts the responsibility for self-guidance. As she leaves one man and then the other, she travels the two existences of the child of grace and the child of nature.

—Richard Benvenuto, "The Child of Nature, the Child of Grace, and the Unresolved Conflict of *Jane Eyre*," *ELH* 39, no. 4 (December 1972): pp. 631–633.

[Nina Auerbach, a professor of English at the University of Pennsylvania, is one of the leading feminist critics of our time. Among her books are *Communities of Women* (1978), *Romantic Imprisonment* (1985), and *Private Theatricals: The Lives of the Victorians* (1990). In this extract, Auerbach finds that Rochester and his residence of Thornfield are reflections of Jane Eyre's emotional state.]

Thornfield and Rochester are from the beginning a reflection of Jane's inner world. She applies for the position only after Miss Temple has left Lowood, when she feels in herself 'the stirring of old emotions' which had, presumably, been frozen over by Lowood and subdued by Miss Temple. At Thornfield, the fairy-tales of her childhood, associated especially with the red room, seem to come to life: the drawing room seems 'a fairy place,' she approaches Bertha's quarters and thinks prophetically of 'a corridor in some Bluebeard's castle,' she hears Rochester's horse and thinks of 'Bessie's Gytrash.' Jane alone can speak French to Adèle, a language which had ambiguous underground connotations for Charlotte Brontë: she may have associated it with the sudden conflagration of emotion brought about in Brussels by M. Héger, to whom she spoke and wrote only in French. Bertha puts on Jane's wedding veil and looks in her mirror: in the red room, Jane had seen herself in the mirror as 'half fairy, half imp,' and now Bertha's reflection reminds her of 'the foul German spectre—the Vampyre.' Adèle, the sensual child, and Bertha, whose uncontrolled passion has run into insanity, come from Jane's own fire, just as Helen Burns and Miss Temple came from her ice. Thornfield embodies the attraction and the danger of the desires that arise when Miss Temple's restraint is withdrawn; just before Jane flees Rochester's anarchic love for her, she dreams that she is lying once again in the red room at Gateshead.

Away from Thornfield, the world is again obdurate and hostile. Jane arrives in a town that is 'no town . . . but a stone pillar.' The 'sympathies of Nature with man' are withdrawn, though at first she expects still to be cherished by the 'universal mother, Nature':

> I touched the heath: it was dry, and yet warm with the heat of the summer day. I looked at the sky; it was pure: a kindly star twin-kled just above the chasm ridge. The dew fell, but with propitious

softness; no breeze whispered. Nature *seemed to me* benign and good; I *thought* she loved me, outcast as I was; and I, who from man could anticipate only mistrust, rejection, insult, clung to her with filial fondness. Tonight, at least, I would be her guest—as I was her child: my mother would lodge me without money and without price. [My italics]

But on the next night, the sentimental hope that lingers from Thornfield is dispelled by the return of the hostile nature of Lowood and Gateshead: 'my night was wretched, my rest broken: the ground was damp, the air cold; besides, intruders had passed near me more than once, and I had again and again to change my quarters: no sense of safety or tranquillity befriended me. Towards morning it rained; the whole of the following day was wet.' At Moor House, she will refer to nature as a 'stinted stepmother.'

St John Rivers is the emotional alternative to Rochester in a world that seems to generate only extremes of fire and ice. The snow-ice-stone imagery that surrounds him, and his severe Christianity, recall the world of Lowood, Mr Brocklehurst, and hell in-burns. The parallel family structure, two sisters and a brother, even look back to the unyielding Reeds at Gateshead and their 'death-white' landscape. Improbably as Charlotte Brontë handles the incident, it is important to the novel that St John is Jane's cousin, and that Moor House is as close as she comes to arriving at her origins, the home she has inherited. His ice is in Jane as well. When her buried emotions began to stir, Thornfield rose up embodying them; when she forces down her passion in the name of Christian principle, she meets her icy cousin, who is forcing down *his* passion for Rosamond Oliver in order to fulfil his spiritual mission. Even his name, St John, suggests Jane's own potential sanctification. If nature was aroused by Rochester's proposal, Heaven is aroused by St John's: 'All was changing utterly, with a sudden sweep. Religion called—Angels beckoned—God commanded—life rolled together like a scroll—death's gates opening, showed eternity beyond: it seemed, that for safety and bliss there, all here might be sacrificed in a second.' The apocalyptic imagery underlines the fact that the governess Jane always had the potential of becoming a Blakean angel.

Jane's marriage to Rochester at Ferndean and her final home there seem less a synthesis of the two worlds than a partial conquest of one world by the other. The fire of Thornfield is extinguished with Rochester's 'flaming and flashing eyes,' and replaced by motifs from the Lowood-Moor House world: Rochester is 'stone blind,' a 'sightless block,' and Bertha, the source of the fire, is now 'dead as the stones on which her brains and blood were scattered.' Like Lowood, Ferndean is built on an "ineligible and insalubrious site': nature no longer nurtures the self, but is somewhat threatening and tainted. Rochester's unlikely conversion to orthodox Christianity suggests the triumph of the Calvinist God, who has been an anti-life force throughout the novel, over the pagan pantheon of Thornfield: there are 'no flowers, no garden-beds' at Ferndean; it is 'as still as a church on a week-day.' The book does not end with Rochester's love lyrics, but with St John's self-immolating cry to this implacable and unnatural divinity. Despite the apparent victory of Jane's fire over St John's ice, of her 'powers' over his God, his country and Mr Brocklehurst's seem to have triumphed after all. Everything that Rochester represented was crushed with Thornfield, and our final sense of the book is that 'reality' is 'imagination,' broken and blind. Jane, who would not be Rochester's mistress, becomes his governess, and the triumph of this side of her character sends us forward to Lucy Snowe, in whose nature 'the world below' is a more imperious force, requiring an even greater distortion of nature to suppress it.

—Nina Auerbach, "Charlotte Brontë: The Two Countries," *University of Toronto Quarterly* 42, no. 4 (Summer 1973): pp. 333–335.

༺ༀༀ༻

ADRIENNE RICH ON JANE EYRE AND BERTHA ROCHESTER

[Adrienne Rich, a prolific American poet, is also a leading feminist and critic. Among her critical works are *Of Woman Born: Motherhood as Experience and Institution* (1976) and *Compulsory Heterosexuality and Lesbian Experience* (1981). In this extract, Rich asserts that Bertha Rochester, the mad wife of Edward Rochester, is a symbol of what Jane Eyre might become in the patriarchal world of Victorian England.]

It is interesting that the Thornfield episode is often recalled or referred to as if it *were* the novel *Jane Eyre*. So truncated and abridged, that novel would become the following: A young woman arrives as governess at a large country house inhabited by a small French girl and an older housekeeper. She is told that the child is the ward of the master of the house, who is traveling abroad. Presently the master comes home and the governess falls in love with him, and he with her. Several mysterious and violent incidents occur in the house which seem to center around one of the servants, and which the master tells the governess will all be explained once they are married. On the wedding day, it is revealed that he has a wife still alive, a madwoman who is kept under guard in the upper part of the house and who is the source of the sinister incidents. The governess decides that her only course of action is to leave her lover forever. She steals away from the house and settles in another part of the country. After some time she returns to the manor house to find it has burned to the ground, the madwoman is dead, and her lover, though blinded and maimed by the fire, is free to marry her.

Thus described, the novel becomes a blend of Gothic horror and Victorian morality. That novel might have been written by many a contributor to ladies' magazines, but it is not the novel written by Charlotte Brontë. If the Thornfield episode is central, it is because in it Jane comes to womanhood and to certain definitive choices about what it means to her to be a woman. There are three aspects of this episode: the house, Thornfield itself; Mr. Rochester, the Man; and the madwoman, Jane's alter ego.

Charlotte Brontë gives us an extremely detailed and poetically convincing vision of Thornfield. Jane reaches its door by darkness, after a long journey; she scarcely knows what the house is like till the next day when Mrs. Fairfax, the housekeeper, takes her through it on a tour which ends in the upper regions, on the rooftop. The reader's sense of its luxury, its isolation, and its mysteries is precisely Jane's, seen with the eyes of a young woman just come from the dormitory of a charity school—a young woman of strong sensuality. But it is the upper regions of the house which are of crucial importance—the part of the house Jane lives in least, yet which most affects her life. Here she first hears that laugh— "distinct, formal, mirthless"—which is ascribed to the servant Grace Poole and which she will later hear outside her own bedroom door. Here, too, standing on the roof, or walking up and down in the corridor, close to the very door behind which the madwoman is kept hidden, she gives silent vent to those feelings which are introduced by the telling phrase: "Anybody may blame me who likes . . ."

The phrase introduces a passage which is Charlotte Brontë's feminist manifesto. Written one hundred and twenty-six years ago, it is still having to be written over and over today, in different language but with essentially the same sense that sentiments of this kind are still unacceptable to many, and that in uttering them one lays oneself open to blame and to entrenched resistance:

> It is in vain to say human beings ought to be satisfied with tranquility: they must have action; and they will make it if they cannot find it. Millions are condemned to a stiller doom than mine, and millions are in silent revolt against their lot. Nobody knows how many rebellions besides political rebellions ferment in the masses of life which people earth. Women are supposed to be very calm generally; but women feel just as men feel; they need exercise for their faculties, and a field for their efforts as much as their brothers do; they suffer from too rigid a restraint, too absolute a stagnation, precisely as men would suffer; and it is narrow-minded in their more privileged fellow-creatures to say that they ought to confine themselves to making puddings and knitting stockings, to playing on the piano and embroidering bags. It is thoughtless to condemn them, or laugh at them, if they seek to do more or learn more than custom has pronounced necessary for their sex.

Immediately thereafter we are made to hear again the laugh of the madwoman. I want to remind you of another mad wife who appears in a novel of our own time—the woman Lynda in Doris Lessing's *The Four-Gated City*, who inhabits not the upper story but the cellar, and with whom the heroine Martha (like Jane Eyre an employee and in love with her employer) finally goes to live, experiencing her madness with her.

For Jane Eyre, the upper regions are not what Gaston Bachelard calls in the *The Poetics of Space* "the rationality of the roof" as opposed to the unconscious and haunted world of the cellar. Or, the roof is where Jane is visited by an expanding vision, but this vision, this illumination, brings her close to the madwoman captive behind the door. In Lessing's novel the madwoman is herself a source of illumination. Jane has no such contact with Bertha Rochester. Yet Jane's sense of herself as a woman—as equal to and with the same needs as a man—is next-door to insanity in England in the 1840s. Jane never feels herself to be going mad, but there is a madwoman in the house who exists as her opposite, her image horribly distorted in a warped mirror, a threat to her happiness. Just as her instinct for self-preservation saves her from earlier temptations, so it must save her from becoming this woman by curbing her imagination at the limits of what is bearable for a powerless woman in the England of the 1840s.

> —Adrienne Rich, "Jane Eyre: The Temptations of a Motherless Woman" (1973). In *On Lies, Secrets, and Silence: Selected Prose 1966–1978* (New York: Norton, 1979): pp. 96–99.

⊗

NANCY PELL ON *JANE EYRE* AND HISTORY

[Nancy Pell is an American literary critic who, in the following extract, studies the historical focus of *Jane Eyre*. Pell declares that the references to historical revolutions are symbolic of Jane Eyre's own emotional state.]

Two allusions in the novel to actual rebellions in English history suggest Charlotte Brontë's awareness that Jane's struggle for a wider life has significant historical implications. First, after a lesson at Lowood school on tonnage and poundage in the early reign of Charles I, Helen Burns confesses her admiration for the Stuart king.

> "I was wondering how a man who wished to do right could act so unjustly and unwisely as Charles the First sometimes did . . . what a pity it was that, with his integrity and conscientiousness, he could see no farther than the prerogatives of the crown. . . . Still, I like Charles—I respect him—I pity him, poor, murdered king! Yes, his enemies were the worst: they shed blood they had no right to shed. How dared they kill him!"

Jane criticizes Helen, both for her visionary passivity and for her royalist sympathies. "If people were always kind and obedient to those who are cruel and unjust," Jane objects, "the wicked people would have it all their own way: they would never feel afraid, and so they would never alter, but would grow worse and worse." Her resistance to the abuse of power, even the Stuart prerogatives, here clearly places Jane among the regicides. Helen tells her that the theory of retribution she has just described is held only by heathens and savage tribes, but Jane's experience dismisses Helen's received doctrine. To her, loving one's enemies means that "I should love Mrs. Reed, which I cannot do; I should bless her son John, which is impossible." Eventually Jane comes to comprehend the value of self-restraint through the example of Miss Temple, director of Lowood, whose quiet resistance to Mr. Brocklehurst's policies of deprivation has nothing to do with axiomatic stoicism. Jane modifies Helen's quietism with Miss Temple's nurturing concern for body and mind and emerges from her childhood, as Q. D. Leavis points out, with an appreciation for self-discipline as a strategy of psychological warfare.

The second reference to historical revolutionary antecedents is both more subtle and more powerful in its implications. Early in the novel the servant Abbot suspects that young Jane is "a sort of infantine Guy Fawkes"; the passage is echoed later on when Jane has become a school mistress in the village of Morton. She receives a visit from St. John on the occasion of a holiday from her duties on the fifth of November. Although the day is not named, it is the traditional British Guy Fawkes Day. The date is not without ambiguities however. In addition to marking the discovery of the Catholic plot to blow up the Houses of Parliament in 1605, it is also the anniversary of the landing of William and Mary at Torbay in the "Glorious Revolution" of 1688. Thus both violent and bloodless rebellions are juxtaposed on the occasion of Jane's passing from the dispossessed to the possessing class. For during his brief visit, St. John—who knows Jane only as Jane Elliott—looks at a sketch that she has drawn and discovers her true name, Jane Eyre, written on the portrait cover. This disclosure leads to the rediscovery of lost connections between Jane and the Rivers family and establishes her possession of the legacy of twenty thousand pounds from her uncle John Eyre. The repeated image of Guy Fawkes and the ambiguous historical allusions to the Fifth of November thus accompany the moment that unites Jane's past and her future.

—Nancy Pell, "Resistance, Rebellion, and Marriage: The Economics of *Jane Eyre*," *Nineteenth-Century Fiction* 31, no. 4 (March 1977): pp. 405–407.

[Sandra M. Gilbert, a professor of English at the University of California at Davis, and Susan Gubar, a professor of English at Indiana University, wrote a history of women's writing in the nineteenth century, *The Madwoman in the Attic* (1979), followed by a three-volume study of women's writing in this century, *No Man's Land* (1988–94). In this extract from the earlier volume, Gilbert and Gubar study the opening of *Jane Eyre*, which they find representative of the emotional conflicts throughout the novel.]

Unlike many Victorian novels, which begin with elaborate expository paragraphs, *Jane Eyre* begins with a casual, curiously enigmatic remark: "There was no possibility of taking a walk that day." Both the occasion ("that day") and the excursion (or the impossibility of one) are significant: the first is the real beginning of Jane's pilgrim's progress toward maturity; the second is a metaphor for the problems she must solve in order to attain maturity. "I was glad" not to be able to leave the house, the narrator continues: "dreadful to me was the coming home in the raw twilight . . . humbled by the consciousness of my physical inferiority" (chap. 1). As many critics have commented, Charlotte Brontë consistently uses the opposed properties of fire and ice to characterize Jane's experiences, and her technique is immediately evident in these opening passages. For while the world outside Gateshead is almost unbearably wintry, the world within is claustrophobic, fiery, like ten-year-old Jane's own mind. Excluded from the Reed family group in the drawing room because *she* is not a "contented, happy, little child"—excluded, that is, from "normal" society—Jane takes refuge in a scarlet-draped window seat where she alternately stares out at the "drear November day" and reads of polar regions in Bewick's *History of British Birds*. The "death-white realms" of the Arctic fascinate her; she broods upon "the multiplied rigors of extreme cold" as if brooding upon her own dilemma: whether to stay in, behind the oppressively scarlet curtain, or to go out into the cold of a loveless world.

Her decision is made for her. She is found by John Reed, the tyrannical son of the family, who reminds her of her anomalous position in the household, hurls the heavy volume of Bewick at her, and arouses her passionate rage. Like a "rat," a "bad animal," a "mad cat," she compares him to "Nero, Caligula, etc." and is borne away to the red-room, to be imprisoned literally as well as figuratively. For "the fact is," confesses the grownup narrator ironically, "I was [at that moment] a trifle beside myself; or rather out of myself, as the French would say. . . . like any other rebel slave, I felt resolved . . . to go all lengths" (chap. 1).

But if Jane was "out of" herself in her struggle against John Reed, her experience in the red-room, probably the most metaphorically vibrant of all her early experiences, forces her deeply into herself. For the red-room, stately, chilly, swathed in rich crimson, with a great white bed and an easy chair "like a pale throne" looming out of the scarlet darkness, perfectly represents her vision of the society in which she is trapped, an uneasy and elfin dependent. "No jail was ever more secure," she tells us. And no jail, we soon learn, was ever more terrifying either, because this is the room where Mr. Reed, the only "father" Jane has ever had, "breathed his last." It is, in other words, a kind of patriarchal death chamber, and here Mrs. Reed still keeps "divers parchments, her jewel-casket, and a miniature of her dead husband" in a secret drawer in the wardrobe (chap. 2). Is the room haunted, the child wonders. At least, the narrator implies, it is realistically if not Gothically haunting, more so than any chamber in, say, *The Mysteries of Udolpho*, which established a standard for such apartments. For the spirit of a society in which Jane has no clear place sharpens the angles of the furniture, enlarges the shadows, strengthens the locks on the door. And the deathbed of a father who was not really her father emphasizes her isolation and vulnerability.

Panicky, she stares into a "great looking glass," where her own image floats toward her, alien and disturbing. "All looked colder and darker in that visionary hollow than in reality," the adult Jane explains. But a mirror, after all, is also a sort of chamber, a mysterious enclosure in which images of the self are trapped like "divers parchments." So the child Jane, though her older self accuses her of mere superstition, correctly recognizes that she is doubly imprisoned. Frustrated and angry, she meditates on the injustices of her life, and fantasizes "some strange expedient to achieve escape from insupportable oppression—as running away, or, if that could not be effected, never eating or drinking more, and letting myself die" (chap. 2). Escape through flight, or escape through starvation: the alternatives will recur throughout *Jane Eyre* and, indeed, ⟨. . .⟩ throughout much other nineteenth- and twentieth-century literature by women. In the red-room, however, little Jane chooses (or is chosen by) a third, even more terrifying, alternative: escape through madness. Seeing a ghostly, wandering light, as of the moon on the ceiling, she notices that "my heart beat thick, my head grew hot; a sound filled my ears, which I deemed the rushing of wings; something seemed near me; I was oppressed, suffocated: endurance broke down." The child screams and sobs in anguish, and then, adds the narrator coolly, "I suppose I had a species of fit," for her next memory is of waking in the nursery "and seeing before me a terrible red glare crossed with thick black bars" (chap. 3), merely the nursery fire of course, but to Jane Eyre the child a terrible reminder of the experience she has just had, and to Jane Eyre the adult narrator an even more dreadful omen of experiences to come.

For the little drama enacted on "that day" which opens *Jane Eyre* is in itself a paradigm of the larger drama that occupies the entire book: Jane's anomalous, orphaned position in society, her enclosure in stultifying roles and houses, and her attempts to escape through flight, starvation, and ⟨. . .⟩ madness. And that Charlotte Brontë quite consciously intended the incident of the red-room to serve as a paradigm for the larger plot of her novel is clear not only from its position in the narrative but also from Jane's own recollection of the experience at crucial moments throughout the book: when she is humiliated by Mr. Brocklehurst at Lowood, for instance, and on the night when she decides to leave Thornfield. In between these moments, moreover, Jane's pilgrimage consists of a series of experiences which are, in one way or another, variations on the central, red-room motif of enclosure and escape.

—Sandra M. Gilbert and Susan Gubar, *The Madwoman in the Attic: The Woman Writer and the Nineteenth-Century Literary Imagination* (New Haven: Yale University Press, 1979): pp. 339–341.

[John Maynard is a professor of English at New York University and the author of *Browning's Youth* (1977) and *Charlotte Brontë and Sexuality* (1984), from which the following extract is taken. Here, Maynard finds the focus of *Jane Eyre* to be a portrayal of the obstacles in the way of mature sexual awakening.]

Jane's subsequent description of their ten years of life together continues the emphasis throughout the Ferndean scenes on their physical closeness. Jane feels supremely blest just because she is fully Rochester's life as he is hers: "No woman was ever nearer to her mate than I am: ever more absolutely bone of his bone, and flesh of his flesh." They have been knit especially closely by the early years of Rochester's dependence on her sight. Now they share heartbeats and conversation all day long. Few readers, even the most happily married in our divorcing age, will believe such a degree of exclusive mutual company, even between an engaging ex-governess and a man with a West Indian and European past, could be entirely satisfactory. This is a storybook ending, a paradise of satisfied love. The interesting point is that it is love conceived of as exceptionally physical, a meeting of bodies as well as true minds and hearts. Lest there be any question about the potency of this, Jane casually alludes to their first-born, leaving open how many children issued from their fruitful union.

Jane Eyre ends, somewhat unfortunately, with a very brief account of St John's missionary activity and his hope for the next world. If Brontë won't allow Jane, probably rightly in character, any irony over St John's disposal of all earthly joys, she nonetheless concludes the novel as a whole with a clear assertion of loving sexual union. Jane herself has manifestly been brought to a decisive choice between the alternatives of ascetic self-suppression and sexual fulfillment. Yet far more than *The Professor*, the work as a whole also speaks most clearly about the myriad obstacles, within and without the individual, to mature sexual awakening. Brontë uses lesser characters and symbolic structures to indicate the difficulties she sees in sexual openness. She shows how fears, conscious suppressions, and undeliberate repressions work within Jane's mind to drive her into anxiety and, finally, a panicked flight. She even builds into the plot of the book a series of obstacles that suggest her own anxieties: Rochester really is in some sense an illegal seducer; sex has helped drive Bertha mad; Rochester does pay a heavy price for his sins, however much this is qualified and ultimately requited. Because such fears of sexuality become actually incorporated into the world of the tale, they require balancing assertions of sexual growth within the plot, especially the timely elimination of Bertha and the marvelous call to Jane. The same nice balancing of forces of suppression and assertion is at work in the mythic world of the novel's action as in the finer analysis of Jane's psychological response or in the examination of sexual alternatives.

In all cases Brontë comes down finally on the side of sexual initiation—with caution. But the assertion on the side of the life force is far less valuable than the quality of the analysis. Brontë shows us on every level of the novel the complex interweaving strands in sexual life that make it at once so central to experience and so easily miswoven or unraveled. Jane's childhood, her early relations with those loving or unloving to her, her position in the world and her degree of independence, her relative inexperience, her moral and religious values, her sense of belonging to a family, her relation to supportive females or female images, her perception of the uses of sexual energies to different lovers, her need to sacrifice herself or others, all affect her capacity to undergo sexual awakening successfully. Brontë, unlike many of her critics, makes no simple case for how a complex individual functions. She lets Jane tell her tale, reveal her delicate and complicated responses, and challenge us to comprehend sexual experience in its complex totality. The result, for all its occasional naivetés, is one of the finest novels in English and a particularly splendid examination of the process of sexual awakening. Good as the studies of Caroline Vernon's seduction or Elizabeth Hastings's flight from sexuality were, this is miles further along. With tact and infinite delicacy Brontë unfolds and examines the sexual life. For this area of experience, so close to the unconscious world of symbolic language, she needs and finds language rarely drawn upon by as subtle a predecessor in psychological analysis as Jane Austen: strong symbols, dreams, mythic overlays, Gothic plot devices, descriptions of buildings or nature and the seasons. Yet the marvel is that in all this welter of large symbols and emotional signs there is the fundamental focus on the delicate workings of and adjustments to Jane's continuous inner life. She is no vague human counter moving through a turbulent world of symbols, though Lawrence's heroes and heroines sometimes are. Jane remains the center of human complexity around which Brontë's vision of the need for sexual fulfillment and its obstacles focus and concentrate. When we have read the work with the attention it deserves, we feel we have come perhaps as close as we shall in language to the infinitely subtle but not totally inexplicable process of sexual growth.

—John Maynard, *Charlotte Brontë and Sexuality* (Cambridge: Cambridge University Press, 1984): pp. 143–144.

BETTINA L. KNAPP ON THE IMAGERY OF THE RED ROOM

[Bettina L. Knapp is a professor at Hunter College and Graduate Center of the City University of New York and the author of *Liliane Atlan* (1988) and *The Brontës* (1991), from which the following extract is taken. Here, Knapp discusses the imagery of the red-room found at the beginning of *Jane Eyre*.]

The image of the *Red Room,* used symbolically by Charlotte at the outset of the novel, points up the psychologically injurious nature of Jane's early years, from infancy to the age of ten, spent in the home of her aunt, Mrs. Reed, who transfers her own frustrations— blending anger and venom—on the defenseless Jane. The most traumatic of the child's protracted punishments was confinement in the "red room," which she believed to be haunted. No warmth, understanding, or tenderness is received by Jane, who is also taunted and brutalized by Mrs. Reed's three spoiled children—particularly her son, John. Thrust on her own resources, the lonely waif lives the life of an exile. Here is an inward journey, perilous, tremulous, and painful.

That the red-room episode should have occurred at Gateshead, the name of Mrs. Reed's estate, is significant. Onomastically, Gateshead reinforces Jane's psychological condition of alienation and sense of imprisonment in a hopeless situation: a *gate* serves as a barrier preventing any free-flowing communication between the protagonist and the outside world; *head* implies Jane's psychological need to develop the thinking side of her personality while keeping her feeling world in check. She had to function analytically, through her *head* or *mind*, and keep her heart and emotions tightly sealed behind the *gate*.

Her restrictive ambiance not only activated bouts of despair in Jane, but also fired the volatile instinctual realm within her psyche. The hermetic sealing of one part of a person encourages an eventful flaring up of incarcerated forces. So powerful may these excoriating energetic charges become that they can no longer be contained, and ignite in sequences of uncontrollable episodes, with understandably devastating results.

To seek peace of mind, Jane would frequently sit in the window seat in the small breakfast room, drawing the *scarlet* drapery around her and thus shutting herself off from the Reed family. A sequence of metonymies—a cold winter scene with its "leafless shrubbery," its "raw twilight," its "storm-beat shrub," its "ceaseless rain sweeping away wildly before a long and lamentable blast"— reveals her condition of psychological deprivation. Within the relatively protected area, encircled symbolically by a fiery curtain, she was able not only to read her favorite books, but to gaze through the window towards freedom. After the fourteen-year-old John reprimands Jane, "a dependent" without money, for reading one of *his* books, he snatches it and flings it at Jane, who, in her attempt to avoid it, falls and strikes her head against the door. Cut and bleeding, she flashes out verbally: "Wicked and cruel boy! . . . murderer." John informs his mother of the incident and Jane is immediately locked up in the red room.

The "room," an enclosed area, is the locus of Jane's agon or struggle. Psychologically, her imprisonment in the red chamber may be viewed as a testing ground—an initiation—thus giving it ritualistic connotations. Functioning as a secret space, it is within this inner area that the heroine will begin to deal with her fears and learn to confront the vagaries of the life experience. Such a trial, undergone by so many heroines and heroes of past times, if successful, endows an initiate with the strength necessary to step into the next stage of development.

The color red, so horror provoking a hue for Jane, has ritualistic significance when identified with fire, warmth, and blood. Empirically speaking, red/blood is a life-giving and life-sustaining force. Because of Jane's highly religious orientation, red may be associated with the blood sacrifice of Christ in Holy Communion, which allows the initiate to bathe in transpersonal spheres. Red also stands for those earth-factors Jane represses: raw instinct, uncontrolled inner urges, and sexual passion.

—Bettina L. Knapp, *The Brontës* (New York: Continuum, 1991): pp. 144–146.

Biography of
Emily Brontë

Emily Jane Brontë was born on July 30, 1818, at Thornton, near Bradford, Yorkshire. She was the fifth child and fourth daughter of the Reverend Patrick Brontë and Maria Branwell (Patrick later changed his name to Branwell Brontë). Emily's sisters, Charlotte (1816–1855) and Anne (1820–1849), were also writers, as was her brother Branwell (1817–1848) to a more limited extent. In 1820 the family moved to Haworth, where Branwell senior obtained a curacy. The next year Emily's mother died; her sister Elizabeth kept house for the family until she herself died in 1842. Emily briefly attended the Clergy Daughters' School at Cowan Bridge in 1824–25 but thereafter was largely educated at home. Beginning in 1826 the Brontë children, fascinated by some toy soldiers their father had brought home, conceived of an imaginary African kingdom called Angria; later Emily and Anne invented a separate kingdom in the Pacific called Gondal. They all wrote poems and prose sketches about these kingdoms for the rest of their lives.

For a period in 1835 Emily accompanied Charlotte as a tutor at a school in East Yorkshire, but she was unhappy there and quickly returned to Haworth. In 1837 or 1838 she worked as a governess at Law Hill, near Halifax; a house near this school, High Sunderland Hall, is thought by some scholars to be the chief inspiration for *Wuthering Heights*. In 1842, as part of a plan to open a school at Haworth, Emily went to the Pensionnat Heger in Brussels with Charlotte to study languages; but, although she was praised for her intellect and especially her mastery of French, her forbidding manner attracted few pupils.

Returning to Haworth late in 1842, Emily devoted herself to the writing of poetry about Gondal. Much of this poetry is full of the same violent, cruel characters that populate *Wuthering Heights*. In the autumn of 1845 Charlotte discovered a notebook containing this poetry; although Emily was at first highly incensed at the discovery, she was gradually persuaded to let Charlotte seek its publication. In 1846 a collection of verse by Charlotte, Emily, and Anne appeared as *Poems by Currer, Ellis, and Acton Bell* (their respective pseudonyms). Emily wrote only one more poem in her lifetime, for by this time she was at work on her one novel.

Wuthering Heights was written between October 1845 and June 1846 and published in December 1847, again under the pseudonym of Ellis Bell. It was not well received and puzzled most of its readers; many of them regarded it as excessively morbid, violent, and indelicate. In the years since Emily Brontë's death the book has found its readership and a steadily growing reputation. It is now considered one of the masterpieces of nineteenth-century fiction and one of the most original novels in English literature.

It is conjectured that Emily was working on an expanded version of *Wuthering Heights* in the final year or so prior to her death; but this version, if there was one, has not been found. Otherwise, little is known of the final two years of her life. Emily Brontë died of tuberculosis at the age of thirty on December 19, 1848. ❁

Plot Summary of
Wuthering Heights

Emily Brontë's *Wuthering Heights* is a gothic love story set on the desolate moors of northern England at the end of the eighteenth century. The doomed love of the protagonists, Cathy and Heathcliff, erupts with ferocious passion over a period of forty years. Brontë maintains a necessary critical distance from the events through Lockwood, a newcomer from London, who records the story in his diary after hearing it from his housekeeper Nelly Dean. Because many of Nelly's characters are living people whom Lockwood meets during the course of his stay, and because daily life interrupts her tale several times, Brontë also creates a troubling, distorted sense of time. The present world is haunted not only by past events; the novel is also framed by a pair of unresolved ghostly visitations which leave the two most incredulous characters—Lockwood and Nelly Dean—wondering at the spiritual mysteries of Wuthering Heights.

The novel begins with Lockwood's diary entry from the winter of 1801. As a new tenant of the Thrushcross Grange estate, he visits his landlord, Mr. Heathcliff (**chapters one** and **two**). At the estate he is attacked by a pack of dogs and, ungraciously and belatedly, rescued by Heathcliff and a servant, Joseph. His second visit is more interesting; he meets Heathcliff's widowed daughter-in-law, Catherine, and his sullen, illiterate cousin Hareton Earnshaw. He offends them all when he mistakes Catherine first for Heathcliff's wife, then for Hareton's. Next, a sudden snowstorm prevents his departure and he must spend the night.

In **chapter three** Lockwood, having been shown to a small bed-chamber, finds the name, Catherine, carved on the old paneled bed and discovers a fragment of the late Cathy Earnshaw's diary. Her youthful scribblings describe a painful Sunday under the guardianship of her older brother, Hindley. The interminable preaching of Joseph, the servant, memorization of Bible passages, Hindley's anger, and her imprisonment in the washroom make up the familiar pattern of her day. Her writings end; she decides to escape to the moors with her playmate Heathcliff.

Lockwood's sleep is disturbed by nightmares; he dreams that he hears a tree knocking on the window and breaks the glass to tear off a branch. Reaching out into the storm he is grabbed by an ice-cold hand; a child's face appears outside; a voice identifying itself as Catherine Linton begs to be let in. He wakes in terror; his cry rouses Heathcliff whose anguish over the dead Catherine astonishes Lockwood. Heathcliff throws open the windows and tearfully begs Cathy's ghost to enter.

At breakfast the next morning Heathcliff seems transformed from wretched lover to angry, brutish master, roughly upbraiding Catherine, who lashes back in kind. Lockwood leaves the grim household in disgust. He becomes ill on his journey home. In **chapters four** through **thirty** he lies in bed and listens to his housekeeper's story of Wuthering Heights. A servant in the Earnshaw house since childhood, Nelly begins her story with the arrival of Heathcliff when Hindley Earnshaw was fourteen and his sister Cathy was six. Their father returned from a trip to London with a mysterious ragged gypsy child, whom the family first greeted with horror. Grudgingly accepted, Heathcliff, as he was called, became the master's favorite and grew to be Cathy's ally and Hindley's hated enemy.

After the death of the elder Mr. Earnshaw Hindley, now married to a weak and silly woman, takes over Wuthering Heights and immediately cuts off Heathcliff's education, forcing him to work as an indigent farm laborer. Cathy, too, suffers her brother's cruelties, but they only make her friendship with Heathcliff stronger; they become more reckless and more devoted to each other.

One Sunday evening (here in **chapter six** Nelly's story picks up where Cathy's diary ends) Cathy and Heathcliff escape to the moors and sneak up to the neighboring Linton estate, Thrushcross Grange. They observe the spoiled Linton children, Edgar and Isabella, through a window, in the throes of a mutual tantrum. Before the voyeurs can leave, guard dogs attack; one grabs Cathy's ankle and the two are caught. Once inside the house, Edgar recognizes Cathy and the family rush to her aid. Dark, ragged Heathcliff, however, is declared "unfit for a decent house" and thrown out, leaving Cathy surrounded by a doting family.

In this episode Brontë contrasts two distinctive spaces in the novel. Reversing anticipated associations, she describes the cruel unsheltering moor as a savage earthly paradise where Cathy and Heathcliff are free and equal. The Lintons' comfortable parlor, "a splendid place carpeted with crimson and crimson covered chairs and tables," is a site of unhappiness; a wrongheaded, restrictive heaven. When Cathy abandons the moor, her shared world with Heathcliff, the act has biblical connotations, making her choice a fall from innocence.

Cathy is torn between her new friends, the Lintons, and her old friend, Heathcliff. Cathy leads a double life, reckless at home but charming to the Lintons (**chapters seven** and **eight**). Her mask drops one afternoon when Edgar comes courting and Cathy, incited by a jealous Heathcliff and an unindulgent Nelly, takes out her rage on Hareton. Edgar intervenes and she hits him. Shocked, he tries to leave and Cathy breaks into tears. Their fight leads to an open declaration of love.

The day of crisis continues violently. A drunken Hindley threatens Nelly with a carving knife, nearly kills Hareton, and heaps verbal abuse upon Heathcliff, who vows revenge. That evening Cathy confides in Nelly her unhappiness over her engagement to Edgar (**chapter nine**), but laments that to marry the penniless Heathcliff would degrade her. She tells of a dream in which, homesick for earth, she had been flung out of heaven by angels. Marrying Edgar, she tells Nelly, would be like going to that heaven where she would grieve for Heathcliff: "[H]e's more myself than I am! Whatever our souls are made of, his and mine are the same; and Linton's is as different as a moonbeam from lightning, or frost from fire." Her words recall the image from the sixth chapter, of Linton's house as an unhappy, restrictive heaven. Unconventional for its time, her love for Heathcliff is a passionate union of equal souls. As she listens Nelly notices that Heathcliff has overheard from an adjoining room but has left before hearing Cathy's admission of love for him.

Nature acts here as an empathetic participant in the crisis of characters who are themselves so closely associated with the landscape. A summer thunderstorm breaks out and Cathy, distraught when she discovers that Heathcliff is gone, spends the nights looking for him on the moors. Drenched and guilt-ridden, she becomes delirious and falls gravely ill. Nelly briefly recounts the next three years: Cathy recovers and marries, both Linton parents die, Hindley continues his debaucheries, and Nelly goes to live with her mistress at Thrushcross Grange, leaving Hareton in the hands of his negligent father.

In **chapter ten** we learn that the first year of her marriage was happy for Cathy, but that "[i]t was not the thorn bending to the honeysuckles, but the honeysuckles embracing the thorn." Edgar and his sister, Isabella, indulged her every wish. Heathcliff, now prosperous and dressed as a gentleman, returns and shatters this peace. Cathy is overwhelmed with joy, which creates considerable stress between husband and wife. Heathcliff moves in with his old enemy, Hindley, who has lost to him at cards and must settle his debt. Meanwhile, eighteen-year-old Isabella confides to Cathy her infatuation with Heathcliff. Cathy contemptuously asserts to her sister-in-law that Heathcliff is "an unreclaimed creature, without refinement, without cultivation; an arid wilderness of furze and whinstone. I'd as soon put that little canary into the park on a winter's day, as recommend you to bestow your heart on him!" Isabella insists that Cathy is simply jealous, and Cathy then cruelly reveals to Heathcliff her sister-in-law's feelings for him. He admits he detests Isabella's "maukish waxen face," so like Edgar's, but is interested to learn that she is her brother's heir if he dies without a son.

By **chapter eleven** Edgar is trying to throw Heathcliff out of the house. Hareton has turned into a angry, violent child taught by Heathcliff to curse his own father. Nelly finds Heathcliff embracing Isabella and Cathy is called; an argument ensues: Heathcliff accuses Cathy of treating him "infernally" but claims to seek no revenge on her, only upon those weaker than himself. As Edgar runs for reinforcements to eject his houseguest, Heathcliff escapes. Cathy, angry at both men, confides to Nelly that she will hurt them by her own self-destruction: "I'll try to break their hearts by breaking my own." Edgar returns and Cathy explodes into hysterical rage and locks herself in her room. Throughout the novel her diabolical temper, which sends her husband cowering, is matched only by Heathcliff's capacity for rage and vengeance.

After three days Cathy is weak and delirious (**chapter twelve**), telling Nelly of her anguish, thinking herself at the Heights, then realizing her prisonlike married state at the Grange. "Oh, I'm burning!" she cries. "I wish I were out of doors! I wish I were a girl again, half savage and hardy, and free . . . and laughing at injuries, not maddening under them!" She opens the windows and calls for Heathcliff. Meanwhile, Heathcliff has eloped with Isabella.

After two months Cathy is partially restored to health—and she is pregnant. Heathcliff and Isabella return to the Heights: Isabella writes a long letter to Nelly, which she reads to Lockwood in **chapter thirteen**. She tells of Heathcliff's appalling cruelty, and asks Nelly, "Is Mr. Heathcliff a man? If so, is he mad? If not, is he a devil?" Nelly visits and finds Isabella has become as vicious as her husband. Heathcliff forces Nelly to promise to help him to see Cathy.

Heathcliff's speech to Nelly reflects a motif, repeated throughout the novel, of nature describing character through the contrast of wilderness and cultivation. Cathy had likened Heathcliff's soul to the arid wilderness of the moors, while Nelly described the Lintons as honeysuckles, cultivated and fragile. Here Heathcliff proclaims of Edgar's meager love: "He might as well plant an oak in a flowerpot and expect it to thrive, as imagine he can restore her to vigor in the soil of his shallow cares!"

In **chapter fifteen** Cathy and Heathcliff meet and embrace. Cathy, mad with grief because her life cannot include him, falls in faint. That evening she gives birth to a daughter and dies without regaining full consciousness. An angry Heathcliff declares that his only prayer is that Cathy will not rest in peace while he is living. "You said I killed you—haunt me then!" he cries.

Chapter seventeen ends the first half of the novel. Hindley tries to murder Heathcliff and is badly beaten; Isabella taunts Heathcliff, accusing him of murdering Cathy; Heathcliff injures Isabella with a knife; Isabella flees to London and gives birth to a sickly child, named Linton. Within six months Hindley dies, a drunk, so deeply in debt to Heathcliff that his son, Hareton, is forced into dependency on his father's worst enemy. While the first half of the novel has a gothic pitch sustained by its two passionate protagonists, the second half begins with the tone of a fairy tale. In a strange reversal, Heathcliff becomes the vengeful, scheming villain, while a new romantic triangle, uncannily reminiscent of his own, unfolds among the second generation.

In **chapters eighteen** through **twenty** Catherine Linton, Cathy's daughter, grown to adolescence, has both her mother's willful high spirits and her father's gentleness. When her father is called to Isabella's deathbed she rides to the Heights and meets eighteen-year-old Hareton. Edgar returns to the Grange with Isabella's peevish child, Linton, whom Catherine nonetheless dotes upon. Heathcliff claims Linton who, we recall, is the sole heir to Edgar's estate, and Edgar has no choice but to give the child up. Neither Nelly nor Edgar tell Catherine of Linton's whereabouts.

On her sixteenth birthday (**chapter twenty-one**) Catherine, on a walk with Nelly, meets Heathcliff, who cajoles her into visiting Wuthering Heights, where she is overjoyed to find her long-lost cousin Linton, now a self-absorbed and delicate teenager. An illiterate and abused Hareton confides to Nelly his hopes that Catherine and Linton will marry, since Linton may not live to inherit his father's estate. Heathcliff brags to Catherine that he has reduced Hindley's son to the same destitution as Hindley had once reduced him.

Forbidden by her father to have further contact with anyone at the Heights, Catherine and Linton exchange love letters. Several months after Nelly forces her to burn them. Catherine is accosted by Heathcliff, who accuses her of breaking Linton's heart, insisting his son is dying. Catherine decides to visit secretly (**chapter twenty-three**).

By **chapter twenty-seven,** Edgar's health is failing and seventeen-year-old Catherine continues to visit Linton who, crazed with fear, falls limp and Catherine must help Heathcliff to escort him into the house. Heathcliff, in his strongest incarnation of the gothic villain, kidnaps Catherine. He locks the door and slaps her for resisting him and forces her to marry Linton. Catherine escapes, briefly, to return to her dying father. After the funeral Heathcliff arrives to take Catherine back to the Heights to nurse Linton. He tells a horrified Nelly that he had dug up and opened Cathy's coffin. He tells how he has been haunted by her presence since the night of her funeral, when he had first dug up her coffin and heard a distinct sigh at his ear. From that moment he had felt her presence constantly. "And when I slept in her chamber . . ."

he recalls, "I couldn't lie there; for the moment I closed my eyes, she was either outside the window, or sliding back the panels, or entering the room. . . ." The sight of her still unmarred beauty has eased his tortured nerves.

Forced to nurse Linton, Catherine becomes bitter and hostile. The story moves into the present, where Lockwood knows from his own visits to Wuthering Heights the dreary conditions there. His journal now dates from the second week of January 1802: he has recovered from his cold and is determined to leave his isolation for London (**chapter thirty-one**). On a visit to the Heights he finds Catherine mourning for her old life and cruelly taunting Hareton as he attempts to read. The diary leaps eight months to a September visit: Heathcliff is dead and Catherine is engaged to Hareton. Nelly recalls how Heathcliff had become increasingly distracted by an otherworldly force, forgetting to sleep or eat. After wandering the heath through the night, he told Nelly, "Last night I was on the threshold of hell. Today I am within sight of my heaven" (**chapter thirty-three**). That morning Heathcliff is startled by the sight of Catherine and Hareton, who reminds him uncannily of his former self.

Heathcliff's tortuous existence continues; his nocturnal wanderings continue and during the day he locks himself in Cathy's bedroom. After another night of wild storms Nelly breaks into the room to find the windows open; she pulls back the panels and is met with a fierce, unblinking gaze—Heathcliff is dead. To the scandal of the community Heathcliff is buried next to Catherine. Their ghosts are said to walk upon the moors, reunited in this bleak paradise. ✸

List of Characters in
Wuthering Heights

Catherine (Cathy) Earnshaw is the beautiful, passionate, and destructive heroine of *Wuthering Heights*. She finds her soul mate in the dark, brooding Heathcliff but marries a much weaker man and destroys their happiness. She has grown up with Heathcliff, an adopted gypsy child, and their friendship strengthens during an orphaned adolescence under the tyrannical rule of her older brother. Defiant, domineering, and impetuous, Cathy finds a new admirer in the delicate, pampered Edgar Linton, but she grows delirious with grief when a spurned Heathcliff leaves the Heights. Her joy at his return, a year into her marriage to Edgar, is so great that her husband's jealousy is aroused. Violent arguments ensue, and Cathy self-destructively hastens her own end through rage and starvation. She dies in childbirth. Her spirit literally and figuratively haunts the rest of the novel. Heathcliff is tortured by her memory, farmers claim to see her ghost walking the moors, and the narrator himself encounters her frightening dream-figure. Cathy's tragedy also threatens until the last to haunt and repeat itself in the life of her daughter.

Heathcliff is the passionate, vengeful hero of Brontë's novel. His mysterious origin makes him a social outcast among the landed gentry, and his destitute adolescence creates a stoical, calculating temperament. He is Cathy's physical and spiritual equal, but when she accepts Edgar's attentions he deserts the Heights. He returns mysteriously rich and educated, destroying the equilibrium of Cathy's marriage. He elopes with Isabella Linton to destroy her brother, Edgar, and lures Hindley Earnshaw into gambling away his rights to Wuthering Heights. Heathcliff's thirst for revenge is only checked when he senses the imminence of his own death, and with it a final reunion with his ghostly beloved.

Nelly Dean is the housekeeper whose account of the events at Wuthering Heights comprise the body of the narrator's—Mr. Lockwood's—records. She is a sturdy local woman whose commonsensical nature contrasts sharply with the unfettered passions of her subjects. Having grown up in the Earnshaw household and served as Cathy's maid during her marriage, Nelly has a privileged vantage point. She is a keen and critical observer who is not above listening at doors or reading letters. After Cathy's death, Nelly becomes the nursemaid of her daughter, Catherine, and witnesses the twists of fortunes of her new charge. She also witnesses Heathcliff's strange and ghostly death, which contradicts her own rational worldview.

Mr. Lockwood is the secondhand narrator of *Wuthering Heights*: the novel consists of his diary entries during a period as Heathcliff's tenant and records the story he hears from Nelly. Lockwood is a young London gentleman who rents the old Linton estate from Heathcliff and soon grows curious about his misanthropic landlord with the beautiful widowed daughter-in-law. Lockwood is little more than a passive listener, confined to his bed with a cold for most of the novel, yet his impartial facade unsuccessfully hides his admiration for the second Catherine Linton.

Edgar Linton is Cathy's husband. He is a soft, effeminate character, completely in the power of his willful, temperamental wife. He suffers through her rages and illnesses, and when she dies he resigns himself to an isolated life devoted to his daughter. His gentle, timorous nature contrasts entirely with vengeful Heathcliff's passion. His rival destroys his happiness a second time by kidnapping his adolescent daughter, Catherine. The blow is so devastating that Edgar soon dies of grief.

Isabella Linton is Edgar's younger sister. She is a pampered child and a selfish, reckless young woman. When Heathcliff returns, Isabella falls in love with him and they elope, despite her brother's prohibitions and Cathy's serious illness. She is shocked by Heathcliff's cruelty but counters with her own viciousness and flees the Heights on the night of Cathy's funeral, when Heathcliff is overcome by grief. Here she exits the story, moving to the south, giving birth to a son, and then dying twelve years later.

Hindley Earnshaw is Cathy's older brother and Heathcliff's hated enemy. He is jealous of Heathcliff as a child and tries to ruin him once he becomes master of Wuthering Heights. He reduces Heathcliff to abject poverty but falls into bad ways himself after his wife dies. When Heathcliff returns a rich gentleman after several years' absence, Hindley takes him in as a boarder to satiate his greed for gambling. He soon loses his entire estate at cards. Until his death Hindley leads a violent drunken existence indebted to his enemy.

Catherine Linton is Cathy's daughter and the heroine of the second half of the novel. She has both Edgar's gentleness, playing the devoted daughter during an idyllic childhood, and Cathy's willful haughtiness, which manifests itself during her enforced residence at the Heights. Heathcliff kidnaps her and forces her when she is sixteen to marry his dying son Linton. She is soon widowed, orphaned, and stripped of her inheritance, and her miserable life at the Heights begins to parallel that of her mother's under a tyrannical brother. The love she eventually discovers for her rough, illiterate cousin Hareton nonetheless leads to a brighter future.

Hareton Earnshaw is the son of Hindley, Cathy's older brother. When his mother dies soon after his birth, his father becomes a violent drunkard. Hareton grows up angry and unloved. Clear parallels are drawn between the downtrodden Hareton and the sullen young Heathcliff. Hareton's fate threatens to end tragically when the beautiful Catherine Linton arrives at the Heights and scorns her cousin's gestures of friendship. She eventually overcomes her prejudices and Heathcliff dies before he can destroy a union which returns Wuthering Heights to its rightful heir and matches the second generation's true hero and heroine.

Linton Heathcliff is Heathcliff's sickly son, the product of the unhappy union of Heathcliff and Isabella Linton. Raised for his first twelve years by his mother, he is taken to the Heights after her death. Linton is small-minded and cruel despite his physical weaknesses. Terrified of his father and acting only out of self-preservation, he helps Heathcliff to kidnap Catherine and marries her against her will. Linton soon dies, having impressed the reader with his petty selfishness, which stands in sharp contrast to Hareton's rough but well-meaning generosity. ❀

Critical Views on
Wuthering Heights

V. S. Pritchett on Unity with Nature in
Wuthering Heights

[V. S. Pritchett, a British novelist and short story writer, is also an important literary critic. He is the author of *The Living Novel* (1946) and of critical studies of *Balzac* (1973) and *Turgenev* (1977). In this extract, Pritchett argues that the power of *Wuthering Heights* rests in the fact that Brontë rejects civilized society altogether and portrays humanity in unity with nature.]

There is no other novel in the English language like *Wuthering Heights*. It is unique first of all for its lack of psychological dismay. Never, in a novel, did so many people hate each other with such zest, such Northern zest. There is a faint, homely pretence that Nelly, the housekeeper and narrator, is a kindly, garrulous old body; but look at her. It is not concealed that she is a spy, a go-between, a secret opener of letters. She is a wonderful character, as clear and round as any old nurse in Richardson or Scott; but no conventional sentiment encases her. She is as hard as iron and takes up her station automatically in the battle. Everyone hates, no one disguises evil in this book; no one is "nice." How refreshing it is to come across a Victorian novel which does not moralise, and yet is very far from amoral. How strange, in Victorian fiction, to see passion treated as the natural pattern of life. How refreshing to see the open skirmishing of egotism, and to see life crackling like a fire through human beings; a book which *feels* human beings as they feel to themselves.

And that brings us to the more important difference between *Wuthering Heights* and the other English novels of the nineteenth century: Emily Brontë is not concerned with man and society, but with his unity with nature. He, too, is a natural force, not the product of a class. Her view is altogether primitive. Often wild romanticism, the fiery murk of the Gothic revival, threaten to impair her picture; but these literary echoes are momentary. Her spirit is naturally pagan and she appears to owe nothing at all to the general traditions of our novel which has fed upon the sociability of men and women and the preaching of reform. (D. H. Lawrence, who used to be compared with her in the heyday of mysticism twenty years back, is utterly cut off from her by his preaching, by the nonconformist ache.) This isolation of Emily Brontë is startling, and only Conrad and Henry James, in their very different ways, were parallel to her. Here perhaps lies a clue: they were foreigners who were crossed with us. By some Mendelian accident, Emily Brontë seems to have reverted to the Irish strain in the Brontë family and to have slipped back, in the isolation and intense life of the Yorkshire moors, to an earlier civilisation. She is pre-Christian. The vision of the union of man and nature is natural to her. Or rather, as in many writers of split racial personality, one sees two countries, two civilisations, two social histories in conflict.

—V. S. Pritchett, "Books in General," *New Statesman and Nation*, 22 June 1946, p. 453.

DENIS DONOGHUE ON THRUSHCROSS GRANGE AND WUTHERING HEIGHTS

[Denis Donoghue is an Irish-born literary critic and the author of many books, including *The Sovereign Ghost: Studies in Imagination* (1976), *We Irish: Essays on Irish Literature and Society* (1984), and *England, Their England: Commentaries on English Language and Literature* (1988). He is Henry James Professor of Letters at New York University. In this extract, Donoghue compares the differing moral and social values represented by Thrushcross Grange and Wuthering Heights, the former residence standing for rational, civilized values, the latter for imagination and superstition.]

Catherine and Heathcliff are allowed to persevere in their natures; they are not forced to conform to the worldly proprieties of Thrushcross Grange. Conformity is reserved for the next generation. But this is too blunt as an account of the later chapters of the book. The juxtaposition of Wuthering Heights and Thrushcross

Grange is inescapable, but it is not simple. The values of the Grange are social, political, personal, compatible with the emerging England, the cities, railways, the lapse of the old agricultural verities. Wuthering Heights is, in this relation, primitive, aboriginal, Bohemian; it rejects any pattern of action and relationships already prescribed. Finally, Emily Brontë accepts the dominance of Thrushcross Grange, since the new England requires that victory, but she accepts it with notable reluctance. Wuthering Heights has been presented as, in many respects, a monstrous place, but its violence is the mark of its own spirit, and Emily Brontë is slow to deny it. The entire book may be read as Emily Brontë's progress toward Thrushcross Grange, but only if the reading acknowledges the inordinate force of attraction, for her, in the Heights. We mark this allegiance when we associate the Heights with childhood, the Grange with adult compulsions. The Heights is also the place of soul, the Grange of body. Imagination, the will, the animal life, folk-wisdom, lore, superstition, ghosts: these are at home in the Heights. The Grange houses reason, formality, thinner blood. Much of this opposition is directed upon the question of education. Heathcliff is not a reader, Edgar is despised for his bookishness; but, at the end, the new generation resolves its quarrel in a shared book. I take this to mean that you must learn to read if you want to marry and live in the Grange. The young Cathy teaches Hareton to read, and thus redeems him. Emily Brontë endorses the change, but again with some reluctance, as if the Gutenberg civilization, inevitably successful, meant the death of other values dear to her. The end of the book is an image of concord, but we are meant to register the loss, too. This is implicit in the composition of the book. The fiction is Emily Brontë's composition, her assertion, and in a sense her act of defiance—set against the demonstrable success of fact, time, history, and the public world. At the end, Catherine and Hareton are to marry and, on New Year's Day, to move to the Grange. As for Wuthering Heights, another writer would have burnt it to the ground, but Emily Brontë retains it, in a measure. Joseph will take care of the house, meaning the living rooms, "and perhaps a lad to keep him company." As Mrs. Dean says, "they will live in the kitchen, and the rest will be shut up." The tone of this passage makes it clear that much of Emily Brontë's imagination remains at Wuthering Heights, not as a ghost to haunt it, but as a mind to respect it. It has been argued that we are not to choose between the two houses, but rather to hold them together in the mind. At the end, we choose, as Emily Brontë chose, as Cathy and Hareton chose; but we make the choice with reluctance and with a sense of the values which are inevitably lost. Wuthering Heights is not merely the terrible place of Lockwood's visits, not merely the result of rough manners, bad education, a gnarled landscape. Its chief characteristic is that it exists in its own right, by a natural law formulated, as it were, centuries before the laws of man and society. To that extent, it is closer than Thrushcross Grange to those motives and imperatives which, helplessly, we call Nature. That is its strength. We should not feel embarrassed by the violence of the first part of the book; it is neither melodramatic nor spurious. The energy dramatized there has nothing to sustain it but itself: hence its association with the elements, especially with wind, water, and fire, and with animals, dogs, snow. It is linked also to the landscape, the firs permanently slanted by the wind. "My love for Heathcliff," Catherine says, "resembles the eternal rocks beneath—a source of little visible delight, but necessary." The sentence provides a motto for the entire book, the acknowledgment of quality and character followed by appeal to an older law: necessity.

> —Denis Donoghue, "Emily Brontë: On the Latitude of Interpretation," *The Interpretation of Narrative: Theory and Practice*, ed. Morton W. Bloomfield (Cambridge, MA: Harvard University Press, 1970): pp. 131–132.

⊛

ARNOLD KRUPAT ON HEATHCLIFF'S DICTION

[Arnold Krupat is a professor of English and director of American studies at Sarah Lawrence College. He is the author of *For Those Who Come After: A Study of Native American Autobiography* (1985) and *Ethnocriticism: Ethnography, History, Literature* (1992). In this extract, Krupat argues that the development of Heathcliff's diction from gibberish to weariness is a tool Brontë used to convey the wildness of the world inhabited by the characters of *Wuthering Heights*.]

That Miss Brontë might have given us narrators with a more interesting or important style, that she could perfectly well have imagined speech more appropriate than any Nelly and Lockwood can produce is clear from the speech of almost all of the other characters, but foremost from the speech assigned to Heathcliff. Heathcliff's diction is precisely not fixed and unshakable, nor is it fully formed from the start. His style has a certain development throughout the novel.

Heathcliff's first words as a child are described as "gibberish that nobody could understand," and his last words are a curse of sorts. In between are many modulations. Almost always rough and violent, Heathcliff can nevertheless speak politely, even wittily; near the end of his life the roughness and violence begin to alternate with tones of weariness. Heathcliff's voice also has an element of unpredictability largely lacking in Nelly's and Lockwood's; we can guess the words that will accompany his responses to events rather less well than we can guess theirs.

Among the other characters, we may note briefly that Catherine Earnshaw's diction is not fixed either; yet she dies halfway through the book, before we can hear her speak to as many occasions as we would like. Hareton's diction also has a development, but in his case, similarly, we stop hearing the voice—for the book ends—just as its development seems likely to become interesting. These characters, too, tend more to occasional speechlessness than do either Nelly or Lockwood, as if to testify to the possibility that some responses to some experiences may be incapable of verbalization, that the world may not always be manageable—at least not in words. From them we hear speech often as strange as the experience it seeks to deal with.

The point, of course, is that Emily Brontë chose to give us little of Heathcliff's sort of speech and much of Nelly's and Lockwood's. One reason for this ⟨. . .⟩ is that to develop at length a highly distinctive diction consistent with highly distinctive materials is always to some extent to tame those materials. Simply to maintain such a special style (like Melville's or Faulkner's, for example) at length is to assert that strangeness can be contained, shaped, and ordered—or at least survived. But this is not what Emily Brontë wished to do, nor has it been the effect of her method. The effect of what she has done has been to leave the world wild, for it is just the wildness of the world, its untamable strangeness, that all of us have felt in *Wuthering Heights*. To have conveyed a vast, shapeless sense of things in a thing beautifully limited and shaped is the peculiar effect of Emily Brontë's technique. And the chief strategy of her technique is the persistent split between the materials of the book and the style in which they are presented.

—Arnold Krupat, "The Strangeness of *Wuthering Heights*," *Nineteenth-Century Fiction* 25, no. 3 (December 1970): pp. 279–280.

✿

TERRY EAGLETON ON ECONOMICS AND POLITICS IN *WUTHERING HEIGHTS*

[Terry Eagleton is a Fellow of Wadham College, Oxford, and a leading British literary theorist. Among his many works are *Criticism and Ideology* (1976), *Literary Theory: An Introduction* (1983), and *Heathcliff and the Great Hunger: Studies in Irish Culture* (1995). In this extract, taken from his Marxist study of the Brontës, Eagleton asserts that Heathcliff is a disruptive force in the sociopolitical world of Wuthering Heights because he has no well-defined place in the economic system.]

Throughout *Wuthering Heights*, labour and culture, bondage and freedom, Nature and artifice appear at once as each other's dialectical negations and as subtly matched, mutually reflective. Culture—gentility—is the opposite of labour for young Heathcliff and Hareton; but it is also a crucial economic weapon, as well as a product of work itself. The delicate spiritless Lintons in their crimson-carpeted drawing-room are radically severed from the labour which sustains them; gentility grows from the production of others, detaches itself from that work (as the Grange is separate from the Heights), and then comes to dominate the labour on which it is parasitic. In doing so, it becomes a form of self-bondage; if work is servitude, so in a subtler sense is civilisation. To some extent, these polarities are held together in the yeoman-farming structure of the Heights. Here labour and culture, freedom and necessity, Nature and society are roughly complementary. The

Earnshaws are gentlemen yet they work the land; they enjoy the freedom of being their own masters, but that freedom moves within the tough discipline of labour; and because the social unit of the Heights—the family—is both 'natural' (biological) and an economic system, it acts to some degree as a mediation between Nature and artifice, naturalising property relations and socialising blood-ties. Relationships in this isolated world are turbulently face-to-face, but they are also impersonally mediated through a working relation with Nature. This is not to share Mrs Q. D. Leavis's view of the Heights as 'a wholesome primitive and natural unit of a healthy society'; there does not, for instance, seem much that is wholesome about Joseph. Joseph incarnates a grimness inherent in conditions of economic exigency, where relationships must be tightly ordered and are easily warped into violence. One of *Wuthering Heights'* more notable achievements is ruthlessly to de-mystify the Victorian notion of the family as a pious, pacific space within social conflict. Even so, the Heights does pin together contradictions which the entry of Heathcliff will break open. Heathcliff disturbs the Heights because he is simply superfluous: he has no defined place within its biological and economic system. (He may well be Catherine's illegitimate half-brother, just as he may well have passed his two-year absence in Tunbridge Wells.) The superfluity he embodies is that of a sheerly human demand for recognition; but since there is no space for such surplus within the terse economy of the Heights, it proves destructive rather than creative in effect, straining and overloading already taut relationships. Heathcliff catalyses an aggression intrinsic to Heights society; that sound blow Hindley hands out to Catherine on the evening of Heathcliff's first appearance is slight but significant evidence against the case that conflict starts only with Heathcliff's arrival.

The effect of Heathcliff is to explode those conflicts into antagonisms which finally rip the place apart. In particular, he marks the beginnings of that process whereby passion and personal intensity separate out from the social domain and offer an alternative commitment to it. For farming families like the Earnshaws, work and human relations are roughly coterminous: work is socialised, personal relations mediated through a context of labour. Heathcliff, however, is set to work meaninglessly, as a servant rather than a member of the family; and his fervent emotional life with Catherine is thus forced outside the working environment into the wild Nature of the heath, rather than Nature reclaimed and worked up into significant value in the social activity of labour. Heathcliff is stripped of culture in the sense of gentility, but the result is a paradoxical intensifying of his fertile imaginative liaison with Catherine. It is fitting, then, that their free, neglected wanderings lead them to their adventure at Thrushcross Grange. For if the Romantic childhood culture of Catherine and Heathcliff exists in a social limbo divorced from the minatory world of working relations, the same can be said in a different sense of the genteel culture of the Lintons, surviving as it does on the basis of material conditions it simultaneously conceals. As the children spy on the Linton family, that concealed brutality is unleashed in the shape of bulldogs brought to the defence of civility. The natural energy in which the Lintons' culture is rooted bursts literally through to savage the 'savages' who appear to threaten property. The underlying truth of violence, continuously visible at the Heights, is momentarily exposed; old Linton thinks the intruders are after his rents. Culture draws a veil over such brute force but also sharpens it: the more property you have, the more ruthlessly you need to defend it. Indeed, Heathcliff himself seems dimly aware of how cultivation exacerbates 'natural' conflict, as we see in his scornful account of the Linton children's petulant squabbling; cultivation, by pampering and swaddling 'natural' drives, at once represses serious physical violence and breeds a neurasthenic sensitivity which allows selfish impulse free rein. 'Natural' aggression is nurtured both by an excess and an absence of culture—a paradox demonstrated by Catherine Earnshaw, who is at once wild and pettish, savage and spoilt. Nature and culture, then, are locked in a complex relation of antagonism and affinity: the Romantic fantasies of Heathcliff and Catherine, and the Romantic Linton drawing-room with its gold-bordered ceiling and shimmering chandelier, both bear the scars of the material conditions which produced them—scars visibly inscribed on Cathy's ankle. Yet to leave the matter there would be to draw a purely formal parallel. For what distinguishes the two forms of Romance is Heathcliff: his intense communion with Catherine is an uncompromising rejection of the Linton world.

—Terry Eagleton, *Myths of Power: A Marxist Study of the Brontës* (London: Macmillan Press, 1975): pp. 105–107.

[Patricia Meyer Spacks, a professor of English at Wellesley
College, is the author of many books of criticism, including
*Imagining a Self: Autobiography and Novel in Eighteenth-
Century England* (1976), *Desire and Truth: Functions of Plot
in Eighteenth-Century English Novels* (1990), and *Boredom:
The Literary History of a State of Mind* (1995). In this
extract, Spacks argues that, although Heathcliff dominates
much of the action of *Wuthering Heights*, it is Catherine's
adolescent imagination that is victorious.]

Passion, that ambiguously valued state of feeling, dictates the plot
of *Wuthering Heights*, itself an outpouring of a creative passion with
some analogies to the less productive emotion that dominates
Catherine and Heathcliff. The plot in its complexities keeps
escaping the memory: one recalls the towering figure of Heathcliff,
the desperate feelings of Catherine, but easily loses track of the
intricacies through which the characters develop. Catherine and her
brother Hindley, with their parents and their servants, Joseph and
Nelly, inhabit the old house on the moor at Wuthering Heights.
After Catherine's father brings home the mysterious foundling
Heathcliff, the girl and the waif form an intense, rebellious alliance,
weakened when Catherine makes friends with the prosperous and
conventional Edgar Linton and his sister Isabella. Heathcliff,
neglected and brutalized by Hindley after his father's death, dis-
appears; Catherine marries Edgar; Hindley, whose young wife
dies, sinks toward animality. When Heathcliff returns, he encourages Hindley's degradation. Catherine's deep attention still
focuses on Heathcliff; Isabella promptly fancies herself in love
with him. As part of his elaborate revenge on the Lintons and
Hindley, Heathcliff marries Isabella, who soon flees his brutality
but afterwards bears his son, Linton. Catherine dies in childbirth,
leaving the infant Cathy, who as she grows becomes devoted to
her father. After Isabella's death, Heathcliff reclaims his sickly,
petulant son, and tricks Cathy into marrying Linton, imprisoning
both at Wuthering Heights. Hindley has died; Edgar Linton soon
follows him; Cathy's husband Linton dies shortly after her father,
but Cathy remains Heathcliff's victim, as does Hindley's illiterate,
degraded son, Hareton. Heathcliff's desire for victims weakens,

however, as his obsession with the dead Catherine augments; he dies hoping for union with her, leaving Hareton and Cathy to redeem one another through mature love.

Such bare summary ignores the powerful effects achieved through disjunctive narrative and disparate points of view, particularly through the perspectives of the "outsider" Lockwood—narrator, spectator, and listener—and of self-righteous Nelly Dean. But it suggests the central issues of the novel. The grand passion that determines the fate of Catherine and Heathcliff is intense, diffuse (vaguely involving nature as well as individuals), and sterile. We may believe the lovers in their talk of some mystical union more powerful than death, but no earthly union results from their feeling. Their connection literally produces only destruction. Catherine's incompletely heard confession of her devotion to Heathcliff precipitates his exile, which hardens him into a machine organized for revenge. When Heathcliff returns, his initial appearance causes a quarrel between Catherine and her husband; a subsequent visit produces the painful scene of her articulated contempt for Edgar during which she locks the door and throws the key into the fire; conflict over Heathcliff provokes her desperate illness; his insistence on seeing her eventuates in her death. The side effects of this passion, equally disastrous, include the undoing of Isabella. Linton would never have been born were it not for Heathcliff's plotting; but this fertility contains the seeds of its own frustration. He is born only to be used by others, and to die. The survivors issue not from grand passions but from the union of Edgar and Catherine, Hindley and his socially inferior bride; they point toward the future.

But survival is not the highest of values, nor must the reader judge causes by their effects. Results may be irrelevant; or the truly significant results may be too subtle for evaluation. Catherine is, regardless of her death (perhaps partly *because* of it), a triumphant adolescent, her entire career a glorification of the undisciplined adolescent sensibility. Heathcliff, who looks so much more "manly" than Edgar, is as much as his soul mate an adolescent; more important, he is a projection of adolescent fantasy: give him a black leather jacket and a motorcycle and he'd fit right into many a youthful dream even now. Powerful, manly, mysterious, fully conscious of his own worth, frequently brutal, he remains nonetheless absolutely submissive to the woman he loves—if that is the proper verb. Around her he organizes his life. He provides her the opportunity for vicarious aggression, dominating her husband, tyrannizing over her conventional sister-in-law; when he turns his aggression toward her, though, she can readily master him. A powerful man controlled by a woman's power: when she dies, she draws him to her in death.

Heathcliff is partly a figment of Catherine's imagination as well as Emily Brontë's. Catherine's fantasies, far more daring than Emma's, are equally vital to her development. She focuses them on Heathcliff: if he were not there, she would have to invent him. In fact, she *does* invent him, directly and indirectly shaping his being. After his boyhood, he instigates no significant action that is not at least indirectly the result of his response to her. Because of her he goes away, returns, marries lovelessly, destroys Hindley, claims his own son as well as Hindley's, arranges Linton's marriage, finally dies. But Catherine is also controlled by her own creation, her important actions issuing from her bond to Heathcliff.

Although Heathcliff dominates the action of *Wuthering Heights*, and the imagination of its author and its other characters, Catherine more clearly exemplifies what the two of them stand for. Not yet nineteen when she dies, she cannot survive into maturity; Heathcliff, who lasts twice as long, matures hardly more. Both are transcendent narcissists. Catherine explains that she loves Heathcliff "because he's more myself than I am. Whatever our souls are made of, his and mine are the same, and [Edgar] Linton's is as different as a moonbeam from lightning, or frost from fire." Her analogies suggest the ground of her exalted self-esteem. She and Healthcliff share a fiery nature—a capacity for intense, dangerous feeling. The intensity and the danger are both criteria of value; by comparison the purity of the moonbeam, the clarity of frost seem negligible, even contemptible. Hot is better than cold: Catherine has no doubt about that. The heat of her sexuality and of her temper attest her superiority to the man she marries and her identity with the man she loves; her sense of self is the ground of all her values.

—Patricia Meyer Spacks, *The Female Imagination* (New York: Knopf, 1975): pp. 136–138.

Donald D. Stone on the Romantic Setting of *Wuthering Heights*

[Donald D. Stone teaches at Queens College of the City University of New York. He is the coeditor of *Nineteenth-Century Lives: Essays Presented to Jerome Hamilton Buckley* (1989) and author of *The Romantic Impulse in Victorian Fiction* (1980), from which the following extract is taken. Here, Stone maintains that Brontë traverses the same "Byronic terrain" in *Wuthering Heights* later followed by Edward Bulwer-Lytton.]

Whether Emily Brontë intended her hero to be judged from the moral point of view that her sister applied to Rochester in *Jane Eyre* has never been resolved satisfactorily. Charlotte Brontë had no doubt about Heathcliff's "unredeemed" nature, but she suggested in her Preface to *Wuthering Heights* that Emily "did not know what she had done" when she created him, that her sister had acted under the force of a creative inspiration that had rendered her passive during the act of writing. No English novel has inspired such a diversity of interpretations as *Wuthering Heights*; and Heathcliff in particular has been viewed as an anarchic force of nature, a mythic figure thrust into the real world, a Byronic-derived Satanic outcast, a Marxist proletarian-rebel, a representation of the Freudian Id, and a reflection of the heroine's adolescent narcissism. One is tempted to suggest that the novel's popularity is in large part the result of its oblique allusions and its unwritten passages, those dealing, for example, with Heathcliff's origins or motivations, which later readers have interpreted or supplied themselves to suit their own interests. There is much to pity in Heathcliff's youthful deprivation; but as is the case with Bulwer's similarly bereft heroes, there is also something childish about his diabolical antics (such as hanging his wife Isabella's pet dog), something of the smell of Byronic greasepaint about his physiognomy ("A half-civilized ferocity lurked yet in the depressed brows and eyes, full of black fire"). A number of Victorian critics, in consequence, judged Heathcliff and his companions in the novel as representatives of "the brutalizing influence of unchecked passion ... [,] a commentary on the truth that there is no tyranny in the world like that which thoughts of evil exercise in the daring and reckless breast" [anonymous review in *Britannia*]. In this reading, Heathcliff is analogous to Bertha in *Jane Eyre*: not a hero, but a warning example of the self-destructiveness of the unregulated will. But where Charlotte Brontë deliberately put her characters into a moral context, her sister seems to have thought less in terms of conventional morality than of aesthetic logic—of the relations of her characters to literature rather than to life.

One is tempted to say that *Wuthering Heights* is the Bulwer-Lytton novel that Bulwer himself lacked the genius to write. It has many of Bulwer's stocks in trade: self-willed characters, supernatural occurrences, charged romantic landscapes, a love that transcends death. Within a Bulwer novel the description of Heathcliff's rage following Cathy's death would seem appropriate and properly absurd: "He dashed his head against the knotted trunk; and, lifting his eyes, howled, not like a man, but like a savage beast getting goaded to death with knives and spears." (One recalls the similarly thwarted Castruccio Cesarini's mad fits, in *Ernest Maltrevers*, or the desolation of Falkland after Lady Mandeville's death.) Emily Brontë's triumph was that she went over the same Byronic terrain—"a perfect misanthropist's heaven," as Lockwood describes it—as that followed by Bulwer, and yet avoided making her story seem like the stuff of parody. Bulwer's fiction proves that *Wuthering Heights* is not the great romantic exception among English novels, as was once thought to be the case; yet Emily Brontë had a sense of humor and a conviction that were denied Bulwer. However literary her characters may be in their origins, she believed in them sufficiently to make later readers accept their melodramatic rantings as the echoes of some primal force of reality.

—Donald D. Stone, *The Romantic Impulse in Victorian Fiction* (Cambridge, MA: Harvard University Press, 1980): pp. 42–43.

[Stevie Davies is a British critic and author of *Emily Brontë*
(1988), *Milton* (1991), and *Emily Brontë: Heretic* (1994).
In this extract, taken from her earlier book on Emily
Brontë, Davies believes that the architecture of Catherine's
bedroom is a parable of the conception of reality
embodied by the novel.]

When the principal narrator of *Wuthering Heights*, Lockwood, has
to spend the night at the Heights, he is led in to a room which in
its turn contains a smaller room. This is the clothes-press in which
the elder Catherine had slept as a child. To get in, he has to slide away
the side-panel. Inside this womb- or tomb-like place, he finds a
window, upon whose ledge are a few old, mildewed books, and the
three scratched names—*Catherine Earnshaw, Catherine Heathcliff,
Catherine Linton.* Lockwood is a constitutional voyeur; he cannot
help climbing in and peering round at other people's business. In
telling the story, he provides the framed window of his mind in
order that we too can scrutinize certain secret places. Lockwood
himself is glad of the privacy of the press, feeling 'secure against the
vigilance of Heathcliff, and everyone else'. This is not surprising
in view of the fact that, in attempting a getaway from the unwel-
coming inhabitants of the Heights, he has just been set on by
'two hairy monsters' named as the dogs Gnasher and Wolf, causing
him to emit an outburst of choice and unexpected oaths, and an
undignified nose-bleed, to the amusement of his host. Lockwood
feels so sorely ill-used that he is able to compare himself in his
sufferings with no less a person than King Lear on the heath.

The architecture of the dead Catherine's bedroom, with its
window-within-a-room-within-a-room, and Lockwood peering
about inside, is like a parable of the conception of reality which
the novel enacts. Reality for Emily Brontë is intricately relativistic.
She raises the familiar premise that life is a mesh of anecdotes,
which can be related on the 'I said to her and she said to me' principle, to the status of a philosophical system. The author never tells
you what to think, or how to interpret the material which comes
filtered through so many people's inset dreams, anecdotes, letters,
hieroglyphs, diaries, snatches of song, reminiscences, inscriptions
on houses and signposts. You have to draw deductions as you do

in life itself, whose riddles and clues no authority can conclusively solve, and it is just to be hoped that you will be a little less idiotic than Lockwood, rather less sententious than Nelly, in coming to your conclusions. *Wuthering Heights* rudely mocks its reader. Equally it haunts her or him. Like the bits of diary which Lockwood is able to decipher in the press, Emily Brontë does not offer her book as a fictitious means of bridging the gap between present and past: she reclaims only fragments, leaving us to guess or dream the rest, so that we feel the presence of the elder Catherine's childhood and of her survival after death with the most vivid certainty, yet are not given the slightest conclusive evidence for that survival. Lockwood as a 'reader' of these experiences is not so different from ourselves reading and trying to make sense of the fragments he pieces together, despite the fact that we are encouraged to laugh at him. With his vision framed by his own inadequacies, which are legion, Lockwood (trying to get further and further in to the true story of the Heights) only has access to a framed reality, and cannot know what to call interior, and what exterior—appearance or reality—since every 'inside' place seems to enclose and therefore be displaced upsettingly by yet another 'inside'. For within the closet are books. Inside the books is the elder Catherine's fragmentary diary, scrawled down the margins of the New Testament. This is Catherine's own testament, like a window into the past through which we can glimpse only odd views and catch scraps of conversation (as in Emily's and Anne's own diary-papers). Worryingly, there seem to be three Catherines, each with a different surname: the 'characters'—a fruitful pun suggesting both individuals and handwriting—are baffling, and seem maliciously capable of raising spectres, for when Lockwood nods off the air seems to swarm with Catherines, and he jerks hurriedly awake. By the end of the novel we have solved the riddle of the three Catherines, Earnshaw marrying Linton, begetting a Linton who will marry a Heathcliff, but by the end we have travelled on to a last and first Catherine: the younger Cathy who in a new testament returns to the old in marrying an Earnshaw. The cycle is riddling and confusing, even when we know the answer.

—Stevie Davies, *Emily Brontë: The Artist as a Free Woman* (Manchester, UK: Carcanet Press, 1983): pp. 114–115.

[Robert M. Polhemus, a professor of English at Stanford
University, is the author of *The Changing World of Anthony
Trollope* (1968), *Comic Faith: The Great Comic Tradition
from Austen to Joyce* (1980), and *Erotic Faith: Being in Love
from Jane Austen to D. H. Lawrence* (1990), from which the
following extract is taken. Here, Polhemus notes the prevalence of death in *Wuthering Heights* and believes that the
characters attempt to defeat it by love or eroticism.]

What happens to you after you die? Many people find that religious
faith helps them face that question without falling into despair.
Desire for transcendence, not just of the self but of the self's mor-
tality, has motivated the will to faith since the first syllable of
recorded time; and, if love is a faith, we ought to find that some of
its devotees see it as a hope in confronting—or avoiding—the
problem of personal death and annihilated consciousness. Death
haunts Emily Brontë's *Wuthering Heights*, as it so terribly haunted
the Brontë family, and in its pages she imagines a mystical, passionate calling as a way of facing the immanent and imminent
mortal agony. The book, as earthy a piece of Victorian fiction as
there is, grounds grand romantic passion in the gross texture of
everyday life. Nevertheless, it is a crucial text of mystical erotic
vocation, raising and forcing most of the critical issues that swirl
about romantic love in the post-Renaissance era.

Emily Brontë's characters talk repeatedly about afterlife. No
novelist's imagination has ever bound love and death more closely
together, and no nineteenth-century writer more clearly shows
the relation between the menace of unredeemed, meaningless
death and the rise of popular faith in romantic love. Hating and
fearing death, people have often professed to welcome it as a
release into eternal joy. If you are good, you may go to heaven
when you die; you may find "peace." Some form of that idea has
been a traditional solace of religion. In one of her famous
speeches, Catherine Earnshaw, to the chagrin of conventional
Nelly Dean, rejects such orthodoxy. "If I were in heaven, Nelly, I
should be extremely miserable. . . . I dreamt, once, that I was
there. . . . heaven did not seem to be my home; and I broke my
heart with weeping to come back to earth; and the angels were

so angry that they flung me out, into the middle of the heath on the top of Wuthering Heights; . . . That will do to explain my secret." It will do also to explain the novel's title: "Wuthering Heights" means the rejection of heaven. Reject heaven and you reject angels—even angels-in-the-house. We have here the complaint of romantic individualism that Christian heaven—theocratic authority called bliss and made perpetual—does not seem to be an inviting place or a satisfactory consolation for death.

But it is one thing for advanced poets like Blake, Byron, and Shelley to side with Satan's rebellion against heaven, and another for a Yorkshire parson's daughter to find the dogma of afterlife wanting. We are confronting a growing crisis for orthodox faith. *Wuthering Heights* is filled with a religious urgency—unprecedented in British novels—to imagine a faith that might replace the old. Cathy's "secret" is blasphemous, and Emily Brontë's secret, in the novel, is the raging heresy that has become common in modern life: redemption, if it is possible, lies in personal desire, imaginative power, and love. Nobody else's heaven is good enough. Echoing Cathy, Heathcliff says late in the book, "I have nearly attained *my* heaven; and that of others is altogether unvalued and uncoveted by me!" Even Cathy II and young Linton imagine their own ideas of the perfect heaven. The hope for salvation becomes a matter of eroticized private enterprise.

Faith tries to reconcile what, to reason, is irreconcilable. Consciousness of death and of the self defines us as human, and yet human beings try to deny the death of the self. Catherine and Heathcliff have faith in their vocation of being in love with one another. Says she, "If all else perished, and *he* remained, I should still continue to be; and, if all else remained, and he were annihilated, the Universe would turn to a mighty stranger. I should not seem a part of it." He cries that "nothing"—not "death," not "God or Satan"—has the strength to part them. They both believe that they have their being in the other, as Christians, Jews, and Moslems believe that they have their being in God. Look at the mystical passion of these two: devotion to shared experience and intimacy with the other; willingness to suffer anything, up to, and including, death, for the sake of this connection; ecstatic expression; mutilation of both social custom and the flesh; and mania for self-transcendence through the other. That passion is a way of overcoming the threat of death and the separateness of existence. Their calling is to *be* the other; and that calling, mad and destructive as it sometimes seems, is religious.

Wuthering Heights features the desire to transgress normal limitations, and that desire accounts for its violence and for the eccentric, fascinating flow of libido in it. If we think of the three major acts and areas of erotic transgression for the nineteenth-century imagination—sadism, incest, and adultery—and then consider how the Cathy-Heathcliff love story touches on them, we can see why the novel has had such a mind-jangling effect. It's a very kinky book, replete with polymorphous perversity, sadomasochism, necrophilia, hints of pedophilia, and even a bent towards polyandry, as well as incest and adultery. All this, however, figures in the urge to free the spirit from social conventions, the world, and the galling limitation of the body. That dispersed eroticism, shocking as it is, connects with an underlying drive for the breaking of boundaries—transgression as a means to transcendence.

> —Robert M. Polhemus, *Erotic Faith: Being in Love from Jane Austen to D. H. Lawrence* (Chicago: University of Chicago Press, 1990): pp. 81–83.

⟨♥⟩

SHEILA SMITH ON SUPERNATURALISM AND BALLADRY IN *WUTHERING HEIGHTS*

[Sheila Smith is a Canadian literary scholar. In this extract, she believes that the supernaturalism in *Wuthering Heights* is derived from Brontë's familiarity with traditional ballads, whose paganism and emphasis on passion are reflected in the novel.]

The ballads are fundamentally important to *Wuthering Heights*, especially to the novel's version of the supernatural which records the chief characters' triumphant attainment of a spiritual life, bringing them into accord with each other and with Nature. This life transcends the restrictions of contemporary class prejudices, evades the law (Heathcliff is both metaphorically and, by his cunning, literally outside the scope of the law and with which

Nelly threatens him) and disregards orthodox morality, so often used as an instrument of oppression. Wimberly emphasizes the pagan nature of the ballads: 'The remains of heathendom in folk-song are especially marked . . . the ideas and practices imbedded in British balladry may be referred almost wholly to a pagan culture.' In the novel the pagan world, centred on sexual passion, expressed in the supernatural tale of Heathcliff and Cathy's enduring love, is constantly set against orthodox Christianity, of the routine kind dutifully voiced by Nelly or referred to by Lockwood or Edgar Linton; or the more lurid morality of Calvinistic sects such as Joseph's. Ironically, Joseph, who is constantly inveighing against the pleasures of this life and insisting on the demands of the next, does not convince the reader that he is possessed of the life of the spirit. Joseph's religion is a brand of individualistic materialism, insisting on the return which his outlay of good conduct will ensure him. Despite his continual and vehement references to the Devil, Joseph is not in contact with the supernatural. He remains simply a cantankerous old man, using the terms of his religion to vent his spite against youth, vigour, and love.

In *Wuthering Heights* Emily Brontë revitalizes the literary form of the novel by use of structural devices, motifs, and subjects which properly belong to the oral tradition with which all the Brontë children were familiar, particularly through the agency of Tabitha Aykroyd, the Yorkshire woman who for thirty years was servant in the Brontë household. Elizabeth Gaskell, in her biography of Charlotte, says of Tabby that 'she had known the "bottom," or valley, in those primitive days when the fairies frequented the margin of the "beck" on moonlight nights, and had known folk who had seen them'. ⟨. . .⟩

By adapting in one of the newer genres of the literature of high culture elements of one of the older forms of the literature of folk culture, Emily Brontë extends and develops both Wordsworth's perception of imagination playing upon the familiar to give insight into the human condition, and Coleridge's apprehension of the supernatural as familiar. In *Wuthering Heights* imagination, in the supernatural manifestations, *is* insight, as against the cloudy perceptions of reason and orthodox morality. Her version of reality challenges the materialistic, class-ridden structure of the society of 1847, as Arnold Kettle and Terry Eagleton have suggested. But as

Q. D. Leavis maintains that the allusions to fairy-tales in the novel are a sign of immaturity, so Eagleton argues that the supernatural is a weakness in the book, that Emily Brontë makes a 'metaphysical' challenge to society, but can do this 'only by refracting it through the distorting terms of existing social relations, while simultaneously, at a "deeper" level, isolating that challenge in a realm eternally divorced from the actual'. But, as I have tried to show, the novel's power lies in Emily Brontë's perception of the supernatural as an essential dimension of the actual, and this theme, central in ballad and folk-tale, is expressed by techniques which can be related to those of ballad and folk-tale. She uses the supernatural in her narrative to give direct, dramatic, and objective expression to the strength of sexual passion, as so many of the ballads do. It was this directness which so shocked Emily Brontë's first readers. 'Coarseness' and lack of orthodox morality were charges frequently levelled against the book. Even the perceptive G. H. Lewes, who could not 'deny its truth', found it also 'rude' and 'brutal'. The more obtuse E. P. Whipple, although he acknowledged 'Acton Bell's' (*sic*) 'uncommon talents', objected to 'his subject and his dogged manner of handling it'. Miriam Allott comments that it was Whipple who regarded *Wuthering Heights* 'as the last desperate attempt to corrupt the virtues of the sturdy descendants of the Puritans'. It was left to Swinburne, who had himself been ostracized for setting his poetry against the bourgeois morality of High Victorian society, to make the most perceptive comment on the novel: 'All the works of the elder sister [Charlotte Brontë] are rich in poetic spirit, poetic feeling, and poetic detail; but the younger sister's work is essentially and definitely a poem in the fullest and most positive sense of the term.' For 'poem' read 'ballad'.

—Sheila Smith, "'At Once Strong and Eerie': The Supernatural in *Wuthering Heights* and Its Debt to the Traditional Ballad," *Review of English Studies* 172 (November 1992): pp. 515–517.

Works by
Charlotte Brontë

Poems by Currer, Ellis, and Acton Bell (with Emily and Anne Brontë). 1846.

Jane Eyre: An Autobiography. 1848. 3 vols.

Shirley: A Tale. 1849. 3 vols.

Villette. 1853. 3 vols.

The Professor: A Tale. 1857. 2 vols.

The Adventures of Ernest Alembert: A Fairy Tale. Ed. Thomas J. Wise. 1896.

Poems by Charlotte, Emily, and Anne Brontë. 1902.

Richard Coeur de Lion and Blondel: A Poem. Ed. Clement K. Shorter. 1912.

Saul and Other Poems. 1913.

The Violet: A Poem Written at the Age of Fourteen. Ed. Clement K. Shorter. 1916.

Lament Befitting These "Times of Night." Ed. George E. MacLean. 1916.

The Orphans and Other Poems (with Emily and Branwell Brontë). 1917.

The Red Cross Knight and Other Poems. 1917.

The Swiss Emigrant's Return and Other Poems. 1917.

The Four Wishes: A Fairy Tale. Ed. Clement K. Shorter. 1918.

Latest Gleanings: Being a Series of Unpublished Poems from Her Early Manuscripts. Ed. Clement K. Shorter. 1918.

Napoleon and the Spectre: A Ghost Story. Ed. Clement K. Shorter. 1919.

Darius Codomannus: A Poem Written at the Age of Eighteen Years. 1920.

Complete Poems. Eds. Clement K. Shorter and C. W. Hatfield. 1923.

An Early Essay. Ed. M. H. Spielmann. 1924.

The Twelve Adventurers and Other Stories. Ed. Clement K. Shorter. 1925.

The Spell: An Extravaganza. Ed. George Edwin MacLean. 1931.

The Shakespeare Head Brontë (with Anne and Emily Brontë). Ed. Thomas J. Wise and John Alexander Symington. 1931–38. 19 vols.

Legends of Angria: Compiled from the Early Writings of Charlotte Brontë. Ed. Fanny E. Ratchford and William Clyde DeVane. 1933.

The Professor; Tales from Angria; Emma, a Fragment; Together with a Selection of Poems (with Emily and Anne Brontë). Ed. Phillis Bentley. 1954.

The Search after Happiness. Ed. T. A. J. Burnett. 1969.

Five Novelettes. Ed. Winifred Gérin. 1971.

The Novels of the Brontës (Clarendon Edition). Ed. Ian Jack et al. 1976.

Two Tales. Ed. William Holtz. 1978.

Poems. Ed. Tom Winnifrith. 1984.

Poems: A New Text and Commentary. Ed. Victor A. Neufeldt. 1985.

The Juvenilia of Jane Austen and Charlotte Brontë. Ed. Frances Beer. 1986.

A Leaf from an Unopened Volume; or, The Manuscript of an Unfortunate Author: An Angria Story. Ed. Charles Lemon. 1985.

An Edition of the Early Writings of Charlotte Brontë. Ed. Christine Alexander. 1987.

Works by
Emily Brontë

Poems by Currer, Ellis, and Acton Bell (with Charlotte and Anne Brontë). 1846.

Wuthering Heights. 1847. 2 vols.

Wuthering Heights and Agnes Grey (by Anne Brontë), *with a Biographical Notice of the Authors, a Selection from Their Literary Remains, and a Preface by Currer Bell* (Charlotte Brontë). 1850.

The Life and Works of Charlotte Brontë and Her Sisters. 1872–73. 7 vols.

The Works of Charlotte, Emily, and Anne Brontë. Ed. F. J. S. 1893. 12 vols.

The Life and Works of the Sisters Brontë. Ed. Mrs. Humphry Ward and Clement K. Shorter. 1899–1903. 7 vols.

The Novels and Poems of Charlotte, Emily, and Anne Brontë. 1901–07. 7 vols.

The Works of Charlotte, Emily, and Anne Brontë. Ed. Temple Scott. 1901. 12 vols.

Poems by Charlotte, Emily, and Anne Brontë. 1902.

Poems. Ed. Arthur Symons. 1906.

The Brontës: Life and Letters. Ed. Clement K. Shorter. 1908. 2 vols.

Complete Works. Ed. Clement K. Shorter and W. Robertson Nicoll. 1910–11. 2 vols.

Complete Poems. Ed. Clement K. Shorter and C. W. Hatfield. 1923.

The Shakespeare Head Brontë (with Charlotte and Emily Brontë). Ed. Thomas J. Wise and John Alexander Symington. 1931–38. 19 vols.

The Brontës: Their Lives, Friendships, and Correspondence. Ed. Thomas J. Wise and John Alexander Symington. 1932. 4 vols.

Two Poems: Love's Rebuke, Remembrance. Ed. Fanny E. Ratchford. 1934.

Gondal Poems: Now First Published from the MS. in the British Museum. Ed. Helen Brown and Joan Mott. 1938.

Complete Poems. Ed. C. W. Hatfield. 1941.

Five Essays Written in French. Tran. Lorrine W. Nagel. Ed. Fanny E. Ratchford. 1948.

Complete Poems. Ed. Philip Henderson. 1951.

A Selection of Poems. Ed. Muriel Spark. 1952.

Gondal's Queen: A Novel in Verse. Ed. Fanny E. Ratchford. 1955.

Poems. Ed. Rosemary Harthill. 1973.

The Novels of Charlotte, Emily, and Anne Brontë. Ed. Hilda Marsden, Ian Jack et al. 1976–.

The Brontës: Selected Poems. Ed. Juliet R. Barker. 1985.

Selected Poems (with Anne and Charlotte Brontë). Ed. Tom Winnifrith and Edward Chitham. 1985.

The Complete Poems. Ed. Janet Gezari. 1992.

Poems. Ed. Barbara Lloyd-Evans. 1992.

Works about
the Brontës

Allott, Miriam, ed. *Charlotte Brontë:* Jane Eyre *and* Villette: *A Casebook.* London: Macmillan, 1973.

———. Wuthering Heights: *A Casebook.* London: Macmillan, 1970.

Anderson, Walter E. "The Lyrical Form of *Wuthering Heights.*" *Toronto University Quarterly* 47 (1977–78): 112–34.

Barker, Judith R. V. *The Brontës.* London: Weidenfeld & Nicolson, 1994.

Beer, Patricia. *Reader, I Married Him: A Study of the Women Characters of Jane Austen, Charlotte Brontë, Elizabeth Gaskell, and George Eliot.* New York: Harper & Row, 1974.

Benvenuto, Richard. *Emily Brontë.* Boston: Twayne, 1982.

Berg, Maggie. Jane Eyre: *Portrait of a Life.* Boston: Twayne, 1987.

Bloom, Harold, ed. *The Brontës.* New York: Chelsea House, 1987.

———, ed. *Charlotte Brontë's* Jane Eyre. New York: Chelsea House, 1987.

———, ed. *Emily Brontë's* Wuthering Heights. New York: Chelsea House, 1987.

———, ed. *Heathcliff.* New York: Chelsea House, 1993.

Bock, Carol. *Charlotte Brontë and the Storyteller's Audience.* Iowa City: University of Iowa Press, 1992.

Brick, Allen R. "*Wuthering Heights:* Narrators, Audience and Message." *College English* 21 (November 1959): 80–86.

Buckley, Vincent. "Passion and Control in *Wuthering Heights.*" *The Southern Review* I (1964): 5–23.

Burkhart, Charles. *Charlotte Brontë: A Psychosexual Study of Her Novels.* London: Gollancz, 1973.

Chase, Richard. "The Brontës, or, Myth Domesticated." In *Forms of Modern Fiction: Essays Collected in Honor of Joseph Warren Beach,* edited by William Van O'Connor. Bloomington: Indiana University Press, 1968.

Clayton, Jay. *Romantic Vision and the Novel.* Cambridge: Cambridge University Press, 1987.

Daiches, David. "Introduction." In *Wuthering Heights.* London: Penguin, 1965.

Davis, Stevie. *Emily Brontë: The Artist as a Free Woman.* Manchester, England: Carcanet Press, 1983.

———. *Emily Brontë.* Bloomington: Indiana University Press, 1988.

———. *Emily Brontë, Heretic.* London: Women's Press, 1994.

De Grazia, Emilio. "The Ethical Dimension of *Wuthering Heights.*" *Midwest Quarterly* 19 (Winter 1978): 178–95.

DeLamotte, Eugenia C. *Perils of the Night: A Feminist Study of Nineteenth-Century Female Gothic.* New York: Oxford University Press, 1990.

Dingle, Herbert. *The Mind of Emily Brontë.* London: Martin Brian & O'Keefe, 1974.

Donoghue, Denis. "Emily Brontë: On the Latitude of Interpretation." In *The Interpretation of Narrative: Theory and Practice,* edited by Morton W. Bloomfield. Cambridge: Harvard University Press, 1970.

Dry, Florence Swinton. *The Sources of* Wuthering Heights. Cambridge, England: W. Heffer & Sons, 1937.

Duthie, Enid Lowry. *The Brontë's and Nature.* New York: St. Martin's Press, 1986.

Eagleton, Terry. *Myths of Power: A Marxist Study of the Brontës.* London: Macmillan, 1975.

Ewbank, Inga-Stina. *Their Proper Sphere: A Study of the Brontë Sisters as Early-Victorian Female Novelists.* Cambridge, MA: Harvard University Press, 1966.

Frank, Katherine. *A Chainless Soul: A Life of Emily Brontë.* Boston: Houghton Mifflin, 1990.

Fraser, Rebecca. *The Brontës: Charlotte Brontë and Her Family.* New York: Crown, 1988.

Gaskell, Elizabeth. *The Life of Charlotte Brontë.* 1857. Ed. Alan Shelston. Hammondsworth: Penguin, 1975.

Gezari, Janet. *Charlotte Brontë and Defensive Conduct: The Author and the Body at Risk.* Philadelphia: University of Pennsylvania Press, 1992.

Ghnassia, Jill Dix. *Metaphysical Rebellion in the Works of Emily Brontë: A Reinterpretation.* New York: St. Martin's Press, 1994.

Gilbert, Sandra M., and Susan Gubar. *The Madwoman in the Attic: The Woman Writer and the Nineteenth-Century Literary Imagination.* New Haven: Yale University Press, 1979.

Hinkley, Laura L. *The Brontës: Charlotte and Emily.* New York: Hastings House, 1946.

Homans, Margaret. "Dreaming of Children: Literalization in *Jane Eyre* and *Wuthering Heights*." In *The Female Gothic*, edited by Judith E. Fleenor, 257–79. Montreal: Eden, 1983.

———. "The Name of the Mother in *Wuthering Heights*." In *Bearing the Word: Language and Female Experience in Nineteenth-Century Women's Writing*, 68–83. Chicago: University of Chicago Press, 1986.

Imlay, Elizabeth. *Charlotte Brontë and the Mysteries of Love: Myth and Allegory in* Jane Eyre. Brighton, UK: Harvester Wheatsheaf, 1989.

Keefe, Robert. *Charlotte Brontë's World of Death*. Austin: University of Texas Press, 1979.

Krupat, Arnold. "The Strangeness of *Wuthering Heights*." *Nineteenth-Century Fiction* 25 (December 1970): 269–80.

Kucich, John. *Repression in Victorian Fiction: Charlotte Brontë, George Eliot, and Charles Dickens*. Berkeley: University of California Press, 1988

Leavis, Q. D. "A Fresh Approach to *Wuthering Heights*." In *Lectures in America*, by F. R. Leavis and Q. D. Leavis. New York: Pantheon, 1969.

Linder, Cynthia. *Romantic Imagery in the Novels of Charlotte Brontë*. New York: Barnes & Noble, 1978.

Mathison, John K. "Nelly Dean and the Power of *Wuthering Heights*." *Nineteenth-Century Fiction* 11 (September 1956): 106–29.

Matthews, John T. "Framing in *Wuthering Heights*." *Texas Studies in Literature and Language* 27, no. 1 (Spring 1985): 25–61.

McCarthy, Terrence. "The Incompetent Narrator of *Wuthering Heights*." *Modern Language Quarterly* 42, no. 1 (March 1981): 48–64.

McKibben, Robert C. "The Image of the Book in *Wuthering Heights*." *Nineteenth-Century Fiction* 15 (September 1960): 159–69.

Mitchell, Judith. *The Stone and the Scorpion: The Female Subject of Desire in the Novels of Charlotte Brontë, George Eliot, and Thomas Hardy*. Westport, CT: Greenwood Press, 1994.

Moglen, Helene. *Charlotte Brontë: The Self Conceived*. New York: Norton, 1976.

Moser, Thomas. "What Is the Matter with Emily Jane? Conflicting Impulses in *Wuthering Heights*." *Nineteenth-Century Fiction* 17 (June 1962): 1–19.

Newman, Beth. " 'The Situation of the Looker-On': Gender, Narration, and Gaze in *Wuthering Heights*." *PMLA* 105 (1990): 1029–41.

Oates, Joyce Carol. "The Magnanimity of *Wuthering Heights*." *Critical Inquiry* 9, no. 2 (December 1982): 435–49.

Paglia, Camille. *Sexual Personae: Art and Decadence from Nefertiti to Emily Dickinson.* New Haven: Yale University Press, 1990.

Parkin-Gounelas, Ruth. *Fictions of the Female Self: Charlotte Brontë, Olive Schreiner, Katherine Mansfield.* London: Macmillan, 1991.

Pratt, Linda Ray. " 'I Shall Be Your Father': Heathcliff's Narrative of Paternity." *Victorians Institute Journal* 20 (1992): 13–38.

Showalter, Elaine. *A Literature of Their Own: British Women Novelists from Brontë to Lessing.* Princeton: Princeton University Press, 1977.

Spark, Muriel, and Derek Stanford. *Emily Brontë: Her Life and Work.* New York: Coward-McCann, 1966.

Stevenson, W. H. "*Wuthering Heights:* The Facts." *Essays in Criticism* 35 (1985): 149–66.

Tanner, Tony. "Passion, Narrative and Identity in *Wuthering Heights* and *Jane Eyre.*" In *Teaching the Text,* edited by Susanne Kappeler and Norman Bryson. London: Routledge & Kegan Paul, 1983.

Tayler, Irene. *Holy Ghosts: The Male Muses of Emily and Charlotte Brontë.* New York: Columbia University Press, 1990.

Thomas, Ronald R. *Dreams of Authority: Freud and the Fictions of the Unconscious.* Ithaca, NY: Cornell University Press, 1990.

Visick, Mary. *The Genesis of* Wuthering Heights. 3rd ed. Gloucester, UK: Ian Hodgkins, 1980.

Wallace, Robert K. *Emily Brontë and Beethoven.* Athens: University of Georgia Press, 1986.

Williams, Meg Harris. *A Strange Way of Killing: The Poetic Structure of* Wuthering Heights. Strathtay, UK: Clunie Press, 1987.

Winnifrith, Tom. *The Brontës.* London: Macmillan, 1977.

———. *The Brontës and Their Background: Romance and Reality.* New York: Barnes & Noble, 1973.

———. *Charlotte and Emily Brontë: Literary Lives.* Basingstoke, UK: Macmillan Press, 1989.

Young, Arlene. "The Monster Within: The Alien Self in *Jane Eyre* and *Frankenstein.*" *Studies in the Novel* 23 (1991): 325–38.

Zare, Bonnie. "*Jane Eyre's* Excruciating Ending." *CLA Journal* 37 (1993): 204–20.

Zonana, Joyce. "The Sultan and the Slave: Feminist Orientalism and the Structures of *Jane Eyre.*" *Signs* 18 (1992–93): 592–617.

Index of
Themes and Ideas